2006
Official Playing Rules
of the
National Football League

Roger Goodell, Commissioner

Edited by Larry Upson, Director of Officiating Operations

TRIUMPH
BOOKS

Note: For reasons of space, this edition omits certain supplementary
material ("Approved Rulings" or "A.R.s").

This cover and design treatment copyright © Triumph Books.
Cover photo of Shaun Alexander courtesy of AP/Wide World Photos.
Design by Sue Knopf; page production by Patricia Frey.

This book is available at special discounts for your group or
organization. For further information, contact:

Triumph Books
542 South Dearborn Street, Suite 750
Chicago, Illinois 60605
Tel: (312) 939-3330
Fax: (312) 663-3557

ISBN-13: 978-1-57243-904-7
ISBN-10: 1-57243-904-1

PRINTED IN CANADA

Contents

User's Guide

This edition of the *Official Playing Rules of the National Football League* contains all current rules governing the playing of professional football that are in effect for the 2006 NFL season. Member clubs of the League may amend the rules from time to time, pursuant to the applicable voting procedures of the NFL Constitution and Bylaws.

Any intra-League dispute or call for interpretation in connection with these rules will be decided by the Commissioner of the League, whose ruling will be final.

Because interconference games are played throughout the preseason, regular season, and postseason in the NFL, all rules contained in this book apply uniformly to both the American and National Football Conferences.

Where the word "illegal" appears in this rule book, it is an institutional term of art pertaining strictly to actions that violate NFL playing rules. It is not meant to connote illegality under any public law or the rules or regulations of any other organization.

The word "flagrant," when used here to describe an action by a player, is meant to indicate the degree of a violation of the rules—usually a personal foul or unnecessary roughness—is extremely objectionable and conspicuous.

"Flagrant" in these rules does not necessarily imply malice on the part of the fouling player or an intention to injure an opponent.

Penalties are marked throughout the text with this icon.

New rules and changes to rules are underlined.

The Field

Rule 1

The Field

Section 1 **DIMENSIONS** The game shall be played upon a rectangular field, 360 feet in length and 160 feet in width. The lines at each end of the field are termed End Lines. Those on each side are termed Sidelines. Goal Lines shall be established in the field 10 yards from and parallel to each end line. The area bounded by goal lines and sidelines is known as the Field of Play. The areas bounded by goal lines, end lines, and sidelines are known as the End Zones.

The areas bounded by goal lines and lines parallel to, and 70 feet 9 inches inbounds, from each sideline, are known as the Side Zones. The lines parallel to sidelines are termed Inbound Lines. The end lines and the sidelines are also termed Boundary Lines.

The playing field will be rimmed by a solid white border a minimum of 6 feet wide along the end lines and sidelines. An additional broken limit line 6 feet further outside this border is to encompass the playing field in the non-bench areas, and such broken line will be continued at an angle from each 32-yard line and pass behind the bench areas (all benches a minimum 30 feet back from the sidelines). In addition, within each bench area, a yellow line 6 feet behind the solid white border will delineate a special area for coaches, behind which all players, except one player charting the game, must remain. If a club's solid white border is a minimum of 12 feet wide, there is no requirement that the broken restraining line also be added in the non-bench areas. However, the appropriate yellow line described above must be clearly marked within the bench areas.

In special circumstances (for example, an artificial surface in a multi-purpose stadium) and subject to prior approval from the League Office, a club may omit the 6-foot solid white border during the preseason or later period while football overlaps with another sport, and substitute a single 4-inch white line at what normally would be the outer limit of the solid border (6 feet from the sidelines).

Section 2 **MARKINGS** At intervals of 5 yards, yard lines (3-41-2) parallel to the goal lines shall be marked in the field of play. *These lines are to stop 8 inches short of the 6-foot solid border.* The 4-inch-wide yard lines are to be extended 4 inches beyond the white 6-foot border along the sidelines. Each of these lines shall be intersected at right angles by short lines 70 feet, 9 inches long (23 yards, 1 foot, 9 inches) in from each side to indicate inbounds lines.

In line with the Inbound Lines there shall be marks at 1-yard intervals between each distance of 5 yards for the full length of the field. These lines are to begin 8 inches from the 6-foot solid border and are to measure 2 feet in length.

Bottoms of numbers indicating yard lines in multiples of 10 must be placed beginning 12 yards in from each sideline. These are to be 2 yards in length.

Two yards from the middle of each goal line and parallel to it, there shall be marked in the Field of Play, lines 1 yard in length.

All boundary lines, goal lines, and marked lines are to be continuous lines. These, and any other specified markings, must be in white, and there shall be no exceptions without authorization of the Commissioner. Field numerals must also be white.

Care must be exercised in any end-zone marking or decoration or club identification at the 50-yard line that said marking or decorations do not in any way cause confusion as to delineation of goal lines, sidelines, and end lines. Such markings or decorations must be approved by the Commissioner.

The four intersections of goal lines and sidelines must be marked, at inside corners, by weighted pylons. In addition, two such pylons shall be placed on each end line (four in all).

■ Supplemental Notes

All measurements are to be made from the inside edges of the line marking the boundary lines. Each goal-line marking is to be in its end zone so that the edge of the line toward the field of play (actual goal line) is 30 feet from the inside edge of the end line. Each goal line is to be eight inches wide.

All lines are to be marked with a material that is not injurious to eyes or skin. It is desirable that the yard line markers be flexible in order to prevent injury. No benches or rigid fixtures should be nearer than 10 yards from sidelines.

In league parks where ground rules are necessary, because of fixed conditions that cannot be changed, they will be made by the Commissioner. Otherwise they will be made by mutual agreement of the two coaches. If they cannot agree, the Referee is the final authority after consulting his crew.

Section 3 **GOAL** In the plane of each end line there shall be a centrally placed horizontal crossbar 18 feet 6 inches in length, the top face of which is 10 feet above the ground. The goal is the **vertical plane** extending indefinitely above the crossbar and between the lines indicated by the outer edges of the goal posts.

All goal posts will be the single-standard type, offset from the end line and bright gold in color. The uprights will extend 30 feet above the crossbar and will be no less than 3 inches and no more than 4 inches in diameter. An orange-colored ribbon 4 inches by 42 inches is to be attached to the top of each post.

Note: Goal posts must be padded in a manner prescribed by the league.

Section 4   **PLAYERS' BENCHES**   At the option of the home team, both the players' benches may be located on the same side of the field. In such a case, the end of each bench shall start at the 45-yard line and continue towards the adjacent goal line.

Note: When both benches are so located, chain crew and linesmen are to operate during entire game on opposite side to benches. See 15-4-1.

Section 5   **CHAIN CREW AND BALL BOYS**   Members of the chain crew and the ball boys must be uniformly identifiable as specified by the Commissioner. White shirts are to be worn by members of the chain crew.

Section 6   **SIDELINE MARKERS**   The home club must provide and use the standard set of sideline markers that have been approved by the Commissioner.

Plan of the Playing Field

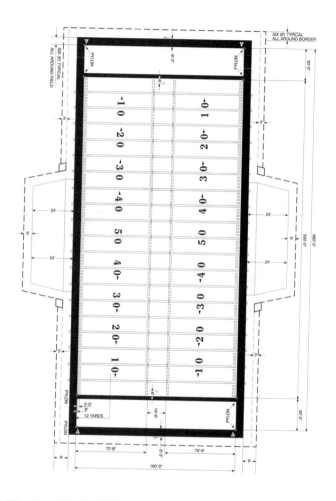

Field Markings

1. The playing field will be rimmed by a solid white border 6 feet wide along the end lines and sidelines. There will be an additional broken yellow line 9 feet farther outside this border along each sideline in the non-bench areas, and such broken line will be continued at an angle from each 30-yard line and pass behind the bench area (all benches a minimum of 30 feet back from the sidelines) at a distance of 6 feet. In each end zone, this broken yellow line is 6 feet from the solid white border. These yellow broken lines are to be 8 inches wide and 2 feet long with a space of 1 foot between them.

In addition, within each bench area, a solid yellow line 6 feet behind the solid border will delineate a special area for coaches, behind which all players, except one player who is charting the game, must remain. Furthermore, a broken white line 4 inches wide and 4 feet long with a space of 2-foot intervals will be marked 3 feet inside the 9-foot restriction line on the sideline, extending to meet the existing yellow broken line 6 feet behind both end zones and at each television box outside the bench area.

2. All lines are to be 4 inches wide, with the exception of the goal line and yellow lines, which are to be 8 inches wide. Tolerance of line widths is plus ¼ inch.

3. All line work is to be laid out to dimensions shown on the plan with a tolerance of plus ¼ inch. All lines are straight.

4. All boundary lines, goal lines, and marked yard lines are to be continuous lines.

5. The four intersections of goal lines and sidelines must be marked at inside corners of the end zone and the goal line by pylons. Pylons must be placed at inside edges of white lines and should not touch the surface of the actual playing field itself.

6. All lines are to be marked with a material that is not injurious to eyes or skin.

7. No benches or rigid fixtures should be nearer than 10 yards from the sidelines. If space permits, they may be farther back.

Inbound Yard Markers

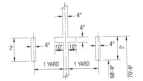

Dimensions for Numerals on the Playing Field

Dimensions for the Directional Arrows

8. Player benches can be situated anywhere between respective 35-yard lines. Where possible, a continuation of the dotted yellow line is to extend from the 30-yard lines to a point 6 feet behind the player benches thereby enclosing this area.

9. A white arrow is to be placed on the ground adjacent to the top portion of each number (with the exception of the 50) with the point formed by the two longer sides pointing toward the goal line. The 2 longer sides measure 36 inches each, while the crossfield side measures 18 inches. The 18-inch crossfield side is to start 15 inches below the top and 6 inches from the goalward edge of each outer number (except the 50).

10. The location of the inbounds lines is 70 feet 9 inches for professional football, 60 feet 0 inches for college football. On fields used primarily by the NFL, the professional inbounds lines should be 4 inches wide by 2 feet long. Alternate college lines, if they are to be included, should be 4 inches wide by 1 foot long.

11. Care must be exercised in any end-zone marking, decoration, or club identification at the 50-yard line, that said marks or decorations do not in any way cause confusion as to delineation of goal lines, sidelines, and end lines. Such markings or decorations must be approved by the Commissioner.

NFL Bench Area Showing Restricting Zones

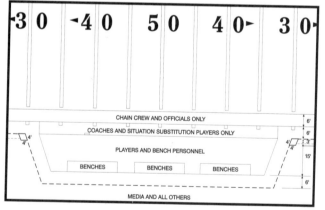

The Ball

Rule 2

The Ball

Section 1 The Ball must be a "Wilson," hand selected, bearing the signature of the Commissioner of the league, Roger Goodell.

The ball shall be made up of an inflated (12½ to 13½ pounds) rubber bladder enclosed in a pebble-grained, leather case (natural tan color) without corrugations of any kind. It shall have the form of a prolate spheroid and the size and weight shall be: long axis, 11 to 11¼ inches; long circumference, 28 to 28½ inches; short circumference, 21 to 21¼ inches; weight, 14 to 15 ounces.

The Referee shall be the sole judge as to whether all balls offered for play comply with these specifications.

Section 2 The home club shall have 24 balls available (domed stadium or outdoor stadium) for testing with a pressure gauge by the Referee two hours prior to the starting time of the game to meet with league requirements. Twelve (12) new footballs, sealed in a special box and shipped by the manufacturer, will be opened in the officials' locker room two hours prior to the starting time of the game. These balls are to be specially marked by the Referee and used exclusively for the kicking game.

A pump is to be furnished by the home club, and balls shall remain with and be returned to the ball attendant prior to the start of the game by the Referee.

In the event a home-team ball does not conform to specifications, or its supply is exhausted, the Referee shall secure a proper ball from visitors and, failing that, use the best available ball. Any such circumstances must be reported to the Commissioner.

In case of rain or a wet, muddy, or slippery field, a playable ball shall be used at the request of the offensive team's center. The Game Clock shall not stop for such action (unless undue delay occurs).

Note: It is the responsibility of the home team to furnish playable balls at all times by attendants from either side of the playing field.

Definitions

Rule 3

Definitions

Section 1   **APPROVED RULING (A.R.)**

An Approved Ruling (A.R.) is an official decision on a given statement of facts and serves to illustrate the intent, application, or amplification of a rule. Supplemental notes are often used for the same purpose (3-32).

An Official Ruling (O.R.) is a ruling made by the Interpretation Committee in the interim between the annual rules meeting and is official only during the current season.

Technical Terms are such terms that have a fixed and exact meaning throughout the code. Because of their alphabetical arrangement in Rule 3, certain ones are used prior to being defined. In such cases they are accented only the first time they are used.

Section 2   **BALL IN PLAY, DEAD BALL**

Article 1   The ball is in play (or Live Ball) when it is:
(a) legally free-kicked (6-1-1 and 2), or
(b) legally snapped (7-3-1).

It continues in play until the down ends (3-7-1; 7-4-1).

Article 2   A Dead Ball is one that is not in play. The time period during which the ball is dead is Between Downs. This includes the interval during all time outs (including intermission) and from the time the ball becomes dead until it is legally put in play.

Article 3   A Loose Ball is a live ball that is not in player **possession**, i.e., any **kick, pass,** or **fumble.** A loose ball that has not yet struck the ground is In Flight. A loose ball (either during or after flight) is considered in **possession** of

team (**offense**) whose **player kicked, passed,** or **fumbled**.
It ends when a player secures possession or when **down
ends** if that is before such possession. (For exception, see
9-1-17-Exc. 3).

Article 4 A Fumble is any act, other than a pass or legal kick,
which results in loss of player possession. The term
Fumble always implies possession. (8-4-2-Exc. 1).

*Note: If a player pretends to fumble and causes the ball
to go forward, it is a forward pass and may be illegal
(8-1-1-Pen. a, c).*

Article 5 A Muff is the **touching** of the ball by a player in an
unsuccessful attempt to obtain **possession** of a loose ball.

*Note: Any ball intentionally muffed forward is a bat and may
be a foul. (3-2-5-g; 12-1-6; 9-1-10-Exc.; 3-14-3-Note 1).*

Touching the Ball refers to any contact. Ordinarily there is
no distinction between a player touching the ball with his
hands or any part of his body being touched by it except as
specifically provided for (9-1-10-Exc., 3-14-3-Note 1).

*Note: The result of the touching is sometimes influenced by
the intent or the location.*

(a) See 6-2-1 and 4 for touching a free kick.
(b) See 6-3-1-Exc. for touching a free kick before it goes
out of bounds between the goal lines.
(c) See 8-1-7 for **ineligible offensive player** touching a
forward pass **on, behind,** or **beyond** the line.
(d) See 9-1-6, 7, 8 for touching a scrimmage kick on or
behind the line, and also 9-1-10 for being pushed
into a kick by an opponent.
(e) See 11-5-1-b for touching a kick during an
attempted **field goal**.
(f) Simultaneous touching by two opponents of a fumble,
pass, or kick is treated under their respective sections.

(g) A Bat or Punch is the intentional striking of the ball with hand, fist, elbow, or forearm. See 12-1-6.

Article 6   A player (5-2-1-S.N. 4) is inbounds when he first touches both feet or any other part of his body, other than his hands, to the ground within the boundary lines (1-1). See (3-20-1) for a player out of bounds.

Note: Unless otherwise stated in the Rules, a player is deemed to be inbounds.

Article 7   A player is in possession when he is in firm grip and control of the ball inbounds (See 3-2-3).

To gain possession of a loose ball (3-2-3) that has been caught, intercepted, or recovered, a player must have complete control of the ball and have both feet completely on the ground inbounds or any other part of his body, other than his hands, on the ground inbounds. If the player loses the ball while simultaneously touching both feet or any other part of his body to the ground, or, if there is any doubt that the acts were simultaneous, there is no possession. This rule applies in the field of play and in the end zone.

The terms catch, intercept, recover, advance, and fumble denote player possession (as distinguished from touching or muffing).

A catch is made when a player inbounds secures possession of a pass, kick, or fumble in flight (See 3-20; 8-1-7-S.N. 5).

Note: It is a catch if in the process of attempting to catch the ball, a player secures control of the ball prior to the ball touching the ground and that control is maintained after the ball has touched the ground.

An interception is made when a pass (forward or backward) is caught by an opponent of the passer.

The term recover indicates securing possession of a loose ball by either the offense or defense after it has touched the ground.

Note 1: If there is any question by the covering official(s) as to whether a forward pass is complete, intercepted, or incomplete, it always will be ruled incomplete.

Note 2: Recovery does not imply advance, unless so stated.

Note 3: If a player would have caught, intercepted, or recovered a ball inbounds but was forced out of bounds, player possession would be granted (8-1-7-S.N. 6).

Section 3 **BLOCKING**

Blocking is the act of obstructing or impeding an opponent by contacting him with a part of the blocker's body.

A Block in the Back is a block that is delivered from behind an opponent above his waist. It is not a block in the back if:

(a) the opponent turns away from the blocker, or
(b) if both of the blocker's hands are on the opponent's side.

A Block Below the Waist is when the initial contact is below the waist with any part of the blocker's body against an opponent, other than the runner, who has one or both feet on the ground. A blocker who makes contact above the waist and then slides below the waist has not blocked below the waist.

Note: If an opponent uses his hands to ward off a block, and the blocker contacts the opponent below the waist, it is not a block below the waist unless the blocker is obviously intending to deliver a low block.

Section 4 **CHUCKING**

Chucking is a means of warding off an eligible receiver who is in front of a defender by contacting him with a quick extension of arm or arms followed by the return of arm(s) to a flexed position, or by maintaining continuous and unbroken contact within five yards of the line of scrimmage, so long as the receiver has not moved beyond the point that is even with the defender (See 12-1-4-Exc. 1).

Section 5 **CLIPPING**

Clipping is throwing the body across the back of the leg of an eligible receiver or charging or falling into the back of an opponent below the waist after approaching him from behind, provided the opponent is not a *runner*.

Note: See 12-2-9 for additional interpretations or restrictions concerning clipping in close line play.

Section 6 **DISQUALIFIED PLAYER**

A Disqualified Player is one who is banished from further participation in the game and must return to his dressing room within a reasonable period of time for any of the following:

(a) flagrant striking, kneeing, or kicking an opponent (12-2-1);
(b) flagrant roughing of a kicker, passer, or any other opponent (12-2-6 and 12-2-12);
(c) a palpably unfair act (12-3-3);
(d) flagrant unsportsmanlike conduct by players or non-players (Rule 13); or
(e) repeat violation of a suspended player rule (5-3-Pen. c).

Note: Disqualified player is not to reappear in his team uniform nor return to any area other than to which spectators have access.

Section 7 DOWN

Article 1 A Down (or Play) is a period of action that starts when the ball is put in play (3-2-1) and ends when ball is next dead (7-4-1).

A down that starts with a snap is known as a Scrimmage Down (3-29).

A down that starts with a fair catch kick is known as a Fair Catch Kick Down (10-1-6; 11-5-3).

A down that starts with a free kick is known as a Free Kick Down (6-1-1 and 6-1-2).

Article 2 A Series of Downs is the four consecutive charged scrimmage downs allotted to the offensive team during which it must advance the ball to a yard line called the necessary line in order to retain possession (7-1-1).

The Necessary Line is always 10 yards in advance of the spot of the snap (which starts the series) except when a goal line is less than 10 yards from this spot. In that case the necessary line is the goal line.

When the offensive team has been in possession constantly during a scrimmage down, the down is counted as one of a series, except as provided for a foul (14-8), and is known as a Charged Down.

The initial down in each series is known as the First Down, and if it is a charged down, subsequent charged downs are numbered consecutively until a new series is declared for either team (7-1-1).

Section 8   **DROP KICK**

A Drop Kick is a kick by a kicker who drops the ball and kicks it as, or immediately after, it touches the ground.

Section 9   **FAIR CATCH**

A Fair Catch is an unhindered catch by any player of the receivers of a free kick or of a scrimmage kick except one that has not crossed the line of scrimmage (3-17-3), provided he has legally signalled his intention of attempting such a catch (10-1-1).

Article 1   The Mark of the Catch is the spot:

(a) where the ball is actually caught by a receiver after a fair catch signal, valid or invalid (10-1-2); or

(b) where the ball is after a penalty for fair catch interference (10-1-4), and after a penalty for running into the maker of a fair catch (10-1-5).

Note: For fair catch kick, see 10-1-6 and 11-5-3.

Section 10   **FIELD GOAL**

A Field Goal is made by kicking the ball from the field of play through the plane of the opponents' goal by a drop kick or a placekick either:

(a) From behind the line on a play from scrimmage; or

(b) During a fair catch kick. See 11-5-3; 3-9; and 10-1-6.

Section 11   **FOUL AND SPOTS OF ENFORCEMENT**

Article 1   A Foul is any infraction of a playing rule. Spot of Enforcement (or Basic Spot) is the *spot* at which a *penalty is enforced.* Four such spots are commonly used. They are:

(a) Spot of Foul—The spot where a foul was committed or is so considered by rule (14-1-1).

(b) Previous Spot—The identical spot where the ball
    was last put in play.

(c) Spot of Snap, backward pass, or fumble—The spot
    where the foul occurred or the spot where the penalty
    is to be enforced.

(d) Succeeding Spot—The spot where the ball would
    next be put in play if no distance penalty were to be
    enforced.

*Note: After a penalty enforcement, the ball is next put in
play at the nearest inbounds line if the penalty enforcement
would leave the ball outside the inbounds line.*

Exception: If a foul occurs after a touchdown and before
the ready for play signal for a Try, the succeeding spot is
the spot of the next kickoff.

*Note: A penalty is never enforced from the spot of a legal
kick from scrimmage (9-1-17).*

An enforcement includes a declination (14-6). See
14-1-5 for definition of basic spot and 3 and 1 rule.

Article 2   Types of Fouls

(a) A Dead Ball Foul (or a subsequent foul) is a personal
    foul (12-2) or unsportsmanlike foul (12-3) that
    occurs after a down ends and before the next snap or
    free kick (14-5). See 14-1-7 to 10, 14-4.

*Note: A dead ball foul is always enforced from the succeed-
ing spot.*

(b) A Multiple Foul is two or more fouls by the same
    team during the same down, unless they are part of a
    double foul (14-4).

(c) A Double Foul is a foul by each team during the
    same down and includes any multiple foul by either
    team, including dead ball fouls (14-3).

Section 12 **FREE KICK**

Article 1   A Free Kick is one that puts the ball in play to start a free kick down (3-2-1, 6-1-1): It includes:

(a) kickoff;
(b) safety kick (6-1-2-a).

Article 2   The Free Kick Line for the kicking team is a yard line through the most forward point from which the ball is to be kicked (6-1-4).

The Free Kick Line for the receiving team is a yard line 10 yards in advance of the kicking team's free kick line (6-1-4).

Section 13 **HUDDLE**

A Huddle is the action of two or more players of the offensive team who, instead of assuming their normal position for the snap, form a group for getting the signal for the next play or for any other reason (7-2-5).

Section 14 **IN TOUCH AND IMPETUS**

Article 1   A Ball is In Touch if:

(a) after it has come from the field of play, it touches a goal line (plane) while in player possession; or
(b) while it is loose, it touches anything on or behind a goal line.

Note: If a player while standing on or behind the goal line touches a ball that has come from the field of play and the official is in doubt as to whether the ball actually touched the goal line (plane), he shall rule that the ball was in touch.

Article 2   A Ball Dead in Touch is one dead on or behind a goal line and it is either a *touchdown*, a *safety*, a *touchback*, a *field goal*, or the termination of a *Try* (11-3), or a loss of down at previous spot (8-1-5).

Note 1: Sometimes a safety, touchdown, or Try (unsuccessful) is awarded because of a foul. In such cases they are penalties. Also note exceptions 8-4-2-Exc. 3, and 8-4-2-S.N.

Note 2: Momentum is an exception to dead in touch. See 11-4-1-Exc.

Article 3   Impetus is the action of a player that gives momentum to the ball and sends it in touch.

The Impetus is attributed to the offense except when the ball is sent in touch through a new momentum when the defense muffs a ball which is at rest, or nearly at rest, or illegally bats:

(a) a kick or fumble;

(b) a backward pass after it has struck ground;

(c) or illegally kicks any ball (12-1-7).

Note 1: If a player is pushed or blocked into any kick or fumble or into a backward pass after it has struck ground, and if such pushing or blocking is the primary factor that sends such a loose ball in touch, the impetus is by the pusher or blocker, and the pushed (blocked) player will not be considered to have touched the ball. See 9-1-10.

Note 2: Momentum is not applicable (11-4-1-Exc.)

Section 15   KICKER

A Kicker is the player of the offensive team who legally punts, placekicks, or dropkicks the ball. The offensive team is known as the Kickers during a kick.

A Receiver is any defensive player during a kick. The defensive team is known as the Receivers during a kick.

Section 16 **KICKOFF**

A Kickoff is a free kick used to put the ball in play:

(a) At start of the first and third periods;
(b) After each Try; and
(c) After a successful field goal (6-1-1-c).

Note: Onside kick (see 6-3-1-Exc.).

If a kicker obviously attempts to kick a ball short and the ball never goes 20 yards, it is defined as an onside kick (this also applies to a safety kick).

Section 17 **LINE OF SCRIMMAGE**

Article 1   The Line of Scrimmage for each team is a yard line (plane) passing through the end of the ball nearest a team's own goal line. The term scrimmage line, or line, implies a play from scrimmage.

Article 2   A Player of Team A is on his line:

(a) when his shoulders face Team B's goal line, and
(b) if he is the snapper, no part of his body is beyond Team B's line at the snap,
(c) if he is a non-snapper, he is not more than one foot behind his line. (For a non-snapper to be on the line of scrimmage, the guideline officials will use is that his helmet must break a vertical plane that would pass through the beltline of the snapper.)

Note: Interlocking legs are permissible.

Article 3   The ball has crossed the scrimmage line (crosses line) when, during a play from scrimmage, it has been run, fumbled, passed, or legally kicked by a Team A player, through the plane of their line and has then touched the ground or anyone behind Team B's line.

Note: At the snap the scrimmage lines are definitely fixed.

After the snap the lines are no longer definite and the Official may construe the line of scrimmage as an indefinite area in the immediate vicinity of the two lines.

Section 18 NEUTRAL ZONE, START OF NEUTRAL ZONE, AND ENCROACHING

The Neutral Zone is the space the length of the ball between the offense's and the defense's scrimmage lines (planes). It **starts** when the ball is ready for play. (See neutral zone infraction, 7-2-2.)

A player is Encroaching (7-2-2) on the neutral zone when any part of his body is in it and contact occurs prior to the snap. The official must blow his whistle immediately.

Exception: The **snapper** is not considered in the neutral zone if no part of his body is beyond Team B's line at the snap (7-2-2).

Note: The Back Judge is responsible for the 40/25-second count with the start of the neutral zone (4-3-9 and 4-3-10).

Section 19 OFFSIDE

A player is Offside when any part of his body or his person is beyond his scrimmage line, free kick line, or fair catch kick line when the ball is put in play.

Exceptions: The **snapper** may be beyond his line provided he is not beyond the defensive line (3-18-Exc.).

The *holder* of a *placekick* for a free kick may be beyond it (6-1-5-b).

The *holder* of a *fair-catch kick* may be beyond it (11-5-3).

The *kicker* may be beyond the line, but his kicking foot may not be (6-1-5-b).

Section 20   **OUT OF BOUNDS AND INBOUNDS SPOT**

Article 1   A player or an official is Out of Bounds when he touches:

(a) A boundary line; or
(b) Anything other than a player, an official, or a pylon on or outside a boundary line.

Article 2   The ball is Out of Bounds when:

(a) the runner is inbounds;
(b) while in player possession, it touches a boundary line or anything other than a player or an official on or outside such line; or
(c) a loose ball touches a boundary line or anything on or outside such line.

Article 3   The Inbounds Spot is a spot 70 feet 9 inches in from the sideline on the yard line passing through the spot where the ball or a runner is out of bounds between the goal lines.

Under certain conditions, the ball is dead in a side zone or has been placed there as the result of a penalty. See 7-3-7 and 7-5-1 to 6.

Note: Ordinarily the out-of-bounds spot is the spot where the ball crossed a sideline. However, if a ball, while still within a boundary line, is declared out of bounds because of touching anything that is out of bounds, the out-of-bounds spot is on the yard line through the spot of the ball at the instant of such touching.

Section 21   **PASS AND PASSER**

Article 1   A Pass is the movement of the ball caused by handing, throwing, shoving (shovel pass), or pushing (push pass) by a runner (3-27-1). Such a movement is a pass, even though the ball does not leave his hand or hands, provided a teammate takes it (hand-to-hand pass).

Note: The term is also used to designate the action of a player who causes a pass as in, "He will pass the ball."

Article 2 It is a Forward Pass if:

(a) the ball initially moves forward (to a point nearer the opponent's goal line) after leaving the passer's hands; or

(b) the ball first strikes the ground, a player, an official, or anything else at a point that is nearer the opponent's goal line than the point at which the ball leaves the passer's hand; or

(c) the ball is handed (regardless of the direction of the movement of the ball) to a player who is in advance of a teammate from whose hands he takes or receives it.

Exception: When the ball is handed forward to an eligible pass receiver (8-1-2) who is behind the line, it is not a forward pass. If the receiver muffs, it is treated as a fumble. (See 8-1-7-S.N. 1 for ball handed forward to ineligible player behind the line.)

Note 1: When a Team A player is holding the ball to pass it forward, any intentional movement forward of his hand starts a forward pass. If a Team B player contacts the passer or the ball after forward movement begins, and the ball leaves the passer's hand, a forward pass is ruled, regardless of where the ball strikes the ground or a player.

Note 2: When a Team A player is holding the ball to pass it forward, any intentional forward movement of his hand starts a forward pass, even if the player loses possession of the ball as he is attempting to tuck it back toward his body. Also, if the player has tucked the ball into his body and then loses possession, it is a fumble.

Note 3: If the player loses possession of the ball while attempting to recock his arm, it is a fumble.

Note 4: A fumble or muff going forward is disregarded as to its direction, unless the act is ruled intentional. In such cases, the fumble is a forward pass (8-1-1) and the muff is a bat (12-1-8).

Article 3 A player who makes a legal forward pass is known as the Passer until the pass ends. The teammates of any player who passes forward (legally or illegally) are known collectively as the Passing Team or Passers.

Article 4 A Backward Pass (8-4-1) is any pass that is not a forward pass.

■ Supplemental Notes

(1) Forward, Beyond, or In Advance Of are terms that designate a point nearer the goal line of the defense unless the defense is specifically named. Converse terms are Backward or Behind.

(2) A pass parallel to a yard line or an offensive player moving parallel to it at the *snap* is considered backward.

(3) If a pass is batted, muffed, punched, or kicked in any direction, it does not change its original designation. However, such an act may change the impetus (3-14-3) if sent in touch or may be a foul (12-1-8, 9).

Section 22 **PILING ON**

Piling On is causing the body to fall upon any prostrate player (other than the runner), or upon a runner after the ball is dead (12-2-7).

Section 23 PLACEKICK

A Placekick is a kick made by a kicker while the ball is in a fixed position on the ground except as provided for a permissible manufactured tee at kickoff (6-1-5). The ball may be held in position by a teammate. See 11-5-4.

Section 24 POCKET AREA

The Pocket Area applies from the normal tackle position on each side of the center and extends backwards to the offensive team's own end line.

Section 25 POST-POSSESSION FOUL

A foul by the receiving team that occurs after a ball is legally kicked from scrimmage prior to possession changing. The ball must cross the line of scrimmage and the receiving team must retain the kicked ball. See 9-1-17-Exc. 3.

Section 26 PUNT

A Punt is a kick made by a kicker who drops the ball and kicks it while it is in flight (9-1-1).

Section 27 RUNNER AND RUNNING PLAY

Article 1   The Runner is the offensive player who is in possession of a live ball (3-2-1), i.e., holding the ball or carrying it in any direction.

Article 2   A Running Play is a play during which there is a runner and which is not followed by a kick or forward pass from behind the scrimmage line. There may be more than one such play during the same down (14-1-12).

■ Supplemental Notes

(1) The exception to a running play is significant only
when a foul occurs while there is a runner prior to a
kick or pass from behind the line (8-3-2, 9-1-17, and
14-1-12).

(2) The statement, "a player may advance," means that
he may become a runner, make a legal kick (9-1-1),
make a backward pass (8-4-1), or during a play from
scrimmage, an offensive player may forward pass (8-
1-1) from behind his scrimmage line, provided it is
the first such pass during the down and the ball had
not been beyond the line of scrimmage previously.

Section 28 SAFETY

A Safety is the situation in which the ball is dead on or
behind a team's own goal line provided:

(a) the impetus (3-14-3) came from a player of that
team;

(b) it is not a touchdown (11-2);

*Note: It is not a safety if a defensive player in the field of
play intecepts a pass or catches or recovers a fumble, backward pass, scrimmage kick, free kick, or fair catch kick and
his original momentum carries him into his end zone where
the ball is declared dead in his team's possession. Instead the
ball belongs to the defensive team at the spot where the ball
was intercepted, caught, or recovered. (11-4-1)*

Section 29 SCRIMMAGE, PLAY FROM SCRIMMAGE

A Scrimmage Down is one that starts with a snap (3-31).
From Scrimmage refers to any action from the start of
the snap until the down ends or if Team A loses possession and Team B secures possession. Any subsequent
action during the down, after a change of team possession, is **Not From Scrimmage**.

Note: The term scrimmage line or line implies a play by A from scrimmage. Line is used extensively for brevity and is not to be confused with side, end, or yard line. Line is also used for free kick line or fair catch kick line. For given reasons, action during a free kick down (6-1), or fair catch kick down, is sometimes referred to as a play not from scrimmage.

Section 30 SHIFT

A Shift is the action of two or more offensive players who (prior to a snap), after having assumed a set position, simultaneously change the position of their feet by pivoting to or assuming a new set position with either one foot or both feet (7-2-5).

Section 31 SNAP AND THE SNAPPER

A Snap is a backward pass that puts the ball in play to start a scrimmage down. The Snapper is the offensive player who attempts a snap. See 7-3-3, for conditions pertaining to a legal snap.

Section 32 SUPPLEMENTAL NOTES (S.N.)

Supplemental Notes (S.N.) are descriptive paragraphs used to amplify a given rule that would otherwise be too cumbersome or involved in its scope or wording.

An Approved Ruling (A.R.) is often used for the same purpose (3-1). Additional Approved Rulings are also found in *The Official Casebook of the National Football League*.

Notes are usually more specific and apply to a particular situation. They are also used to indicate pertinent references to other rules.

Section 33 **SUSPENDED PLAYER**

A Suspended Player is one who must be withdrawn, for at least one down, for correction of illegal equipment (5-3).

Section 34 **TACKLING**

Tackling is the use of hands or arms by a defensive player in his attempt to hold a runner or throw him to the ground (12-1-4).

Section 35 **TEAM A AND B, OFFENSE AND DEFENSE**

Article 1   Whenever a team is in possession (3-2-7), it is the Offense and, at such time, its opponent is the Defense.

Article 2   The team that puts the ball in play is Team A, and its opponent is Team B. For brevity, a player of Team A is referred to as A1 and his teammates as A2, A3, etc. Opponents are B1, B2, etc.

Note: A team becomes Team A when it has been designated to put ball in play, and it remains Team A until a down ends, even though there might be one or more changes of possession during the down. This is in contrast with the terms Offense and Defense. Team A is always the offense when a down starts, but becomes the defense if and when B secures possession during the down, and vice versa for each change of possession.

Section 36 **TIME OUT OR TIME IN**

Article 1   A Time Out is an interval during which the Game Clock is stopped (4-3-1) and includes the intermissions (4-1-1 to 6).

Note: The term Time Out *(general) is not to be confused with a charged team time out, which is specific. (4-3-3).*

Article 2 Time In is the converse (4-3-2) and is also used to indicate when the clock operator is to start his clock.

Section 37 **TOUCHBACK**

A Touchback is the situation in which a ball is dead on or behind a team's own goal line, provided the impetus came from an opponent and provided it is not a touchdown (11-6).

Section 38 **TOUCHDOWN**

A Touchdown is the situation in which any part of the ball, legally in possession of a player inbounds, is on, above, or behind the opponent's goal line (plane), provided it is not a touchback (11-2).

Section 39 **TRIPPING**

Tripping is the use of the leg or foot in obstructing any opponent (including a runner) below the knee (12-1-5).

Section 40 **TRY**

A Try is an opportunity given a team that has just scored a touchdown to score an additional one or two points during one scrimmage down (11-3).

Section 41 **YARD LINE, OWN GOAL**

Article 1 A team's Own Goal during any given period is the one it is guarding. The adjacent goal line is known as its (own) goal line.

Article 2 A Yard Line is any line and its vertical plane parallel to the end line. The Yard Lines (marked or unmarked) in the field of play are named by number in yards from a team's goal line to the center of the field.

Note: The yard line 19 yards from Team A's goal line is called A's 19-yard line. The yard line 51 yards from A's goal line is called B's 49-yard line. (For brevity, these are referred to as A's 19 and B's 49.)

Rule 4

Game Timing

Rule 4

Game Timing

Section 1 **LENGTH OF THE GAME**

Article 1 The length of the game is 60 minutes, divided into four periods of 15 minutes each, with intervals of 2 minutes between the first and second periods (first half) and between the third and fourth periods (second half). During these intermissions all playing rules continue in force and no representative of either team shall enter the field unless he is an incoming substitute. See 13-1-5.

Penalty: For illegally entering field: Loss of 15 yards from succeeding spot (13-1-6, Pen.).

Article 2 The Back Judge is to time the 2-minute intermissions and shall sound his whistle (or signal visibly) at 1 minute and 50 seconds. The Referee shall sound his whistle immediately thereafter for:

(a) play to start; and
(b) play clock operator to start the timing of 25 seconds. See 4-3-10-S.N. 1.

Article 3 The stadium electric clock shall be the official time. The game clock operator shall start and stop the clock upon the signal of any official in accordance with the rules. The Line Judge (15-5-2) shall be responsible for supervision of the timing and in case the stadium clock becomes inoperative, or for any reason it is not being operated correctly, he shall take over the official timing on the field.

Note: Game officials can correct the game clock only before the next play is run, including an untimed down or try.

Article 4 Between the second and third periods, there shall be an intermission of 12 minutes. During intermission, play is suspended, and the teams may leave the field. This is to be timed by the Back Judge. See 15-8-2.

Note: See 13-1-1 to 4 for fouls by non-players between halves.

Article 5   Both teams must be on the field in ample time to kick off at the scheduled time for start of each half. Ample time prior to the start of the game is construed to be at least 15 minutes prior to the initial kickoff in order to ensure sufficient time for proper warm-up. Head coaches must be notified personally before the start of each half by designated members of the officiating crew.

Penalties: For delaying start of half:

(a) **Loss of 15 yards from the spot of the kickoff as determined by Rule 4, Section 2.**

(b) **Loss of coin toss option for both halves, including overtime, and 15 yards if a team is not on the field in ample time prior to the scheduled kickoff as indicated.**

Article 6   Provisions for the sudden death method of determining the winner in case of certain tie scores at the end of game will be found under Rule 16.

Section 2   STARTING EACH PERIOD

Article 1   Not more than three minutes before the kickoff, the Referee, in the presence of both team's captains (limit of six per team, all of whom must be uniformed members of the active list) shall toss a coin at the center of the field. The toss shall be called by the captain of the visiting team or by the captain designated by the Referee if there is no home team. The winner of the toss must choose one of two privileges and the loser is given the other. The two privileges are:

(a) which team is to receive; or

(b) the goal his team will defend.

Penalty: For failure to comply: Loss of coin toss option, both halves, including overtime, and loss of 15 yards from spot of kickoff for first half only.

For the second half, the captain who lost the pregame toss is to have the first choice of the two privileges listed in (a) or (b) unless one of the teams lost its first and second half option under 4-1-5. Immediately prior to the start of the second half, the captains of both teams must inform the Referee of their respective choices.

■ Supplemental Note

(1) When the teams first appear on field for the start of second half, the Referee is to assume a position on one side at the numbers and indicate which team will receive.

Article 2   At the end of the first and third periods, the teams must change goals. Team possession, number of succeeding down, and relative position of the ball on the field of play and of the necessary line remain unchanged.

Section 3   TIMING

Article 1   The game clock operator shall stop the game clock (time out) when upon his own positive knowledge or signal or upon a signal by any official:

(a) the ball is out of bounds (4-3-2-Exc. 3);

(b) a receiver catches after a fair catch signal (10-1-2);

(c) ball is dead in touch;

(d) at end of down during which a foul occurs;

Note: If the game clock was stopped for a foul by either team (whether penalty is accepted or declined), it will be started when the ball is declared ready for play; except when the foul occurred after the two-minute warning of the first half, or the last five minutes of the second half, in which case the clock starts on the snap.

(e) whenever a forward pass is incomplete;
(f) at the time of a foul, for which the ball remains dead or is dead immediately;
(g) upon Referee's signal of the two-minute warning for a half;
(h) when a period expires;
(i) when any official signals a time out for any other reason;
(j) when a kicked ball is recovered illegally and/or surrounded; or
(k) upon the completion of a down involving a change of possession.

Notes: Change of possession includes:

(1) recovery of loose ball by team not putting ball in play;

(2) forward pass interception;

(3) free kick or kick from scrimmage recovered and/or advanced by the receiving team or that goes out of bounds; and

(4) touching of a scrimmage kick by the receiving team beyond the line of scrimmage that is recovered by the kicking team.

Article 2 The game clock operator shall start the clock (time in) after a free kick when the ball is legally touched in the field of play.

Note: Time is not in if:

a) the receiving team recovers in the end zone and makes no attempt to enter the field of play (including running laterally in the end zone);

b) the kicking team recovers in the field of play (Referee's
    timeout under change of possession rule 4-3-7-S.N. 1);
    or

c) the receiving team signals for and makes a fair catch.

Except for a free kick, following any time out (3-36), the
game clock shall be started when the ball is next
snapped.

Exceptions:

1) Except on a change of possession or after the two-
    minute warning of the first half and inside the last
    five minutes of the game, on a play from scrimmage
    whenever a runner goes out of bounds, the game
    clock is started when an official spots the ball at the
    inbounds mark and the Referee gives the ready signal.
2) After the two-minute warning of each half, if there
    is an excess time out, the game clock is started with
    the Referee's whistle, if the clock was running (see
    also 4-3-6-b).
3) After a Referee's time out (4-3-7), the game clock is
    started with the Referee's whistle if the clock was
    running.
4) After a field goal, safety, or touchdown, the game
    clock is next started following the Try as provided in
    4-3-2.

*Note 1: In case of consecutive time outs between downs,
time is in according to the classification of the last time out
(4-3-1-Note 1).*

*Note 2: Consecutive team time outs between downs by
either team are allowed so long as they are not by the same
team and no additional consecutive team time outs can be
taken during the same dead ball period. Such time outs
may follow an automatic time out (4-3-1) or Referee's
time out (4-3-7) and maximum length of the second time out*

will be 30 seconds. An attempt by a team to call its second charged time out during the same dead ball period to "freeze" a kicker prior to a field-goal attempt or Try attempt is unsportsmanlike conduct. See 12-3-1-v.

Article 3   The Referee shall suspend play while the ball is dead and declare a charged team time out upon the request for a time out by the head coach or any player to any official.

If the Referee calls a time out for an injured player, a team time out will be charged if:

(a) the injured player remains in the game; or

(b) players on the field or from the bench attempt to assist the injured player from the field, without being directed to do so by their team physician, trainer, or the Referee; or

(c) the injury occurs after the two-minute warning of either half.

Exceptions:

(1) if a foul committed by an opponent causes the injury, a time out is not charged even if it occurs after the two-minute warning or if the player remains in the game.

(2) if the injury occurs on a play in which there is a change of possession, a time out is not charged even if it occurs after the two-minute warning. The injured player may remain in the game if a time out is called by either team.

Note: Members of both teams may go to the sideline for conference with coaches during an injury time out, but must be ready to play when Referee signals ball in play as soon as treatment is completed or injured player has left the field.

Article 4   Three charged team time outs are allowed a team during each half without a distance penalty (4-3-5). When any team time out occurs, the Back Judge shall start his watch and sound his whistle (or signal visibly) at the expiration of 1 minute and 50 seconds. The Referee shall not blow his whistle for play to start before such a signal from the Back Judge.

Exception 1: Whenever a team time out is called after the two-minute warning in a half, the time out shall last 30 seconds unless more time is required because of an injury or television uses a commercial opportunity.

Exception 2: The Referee may allow:

(a) necessary time to attend to an injured player; or
(b) repair legal equipment.

Note: In the judgement of the Referee, if such a player is not ready for play in a reasonable amount of time, he must be withdrawn.

■ Supplemental Notes

(1) In the case of extended team time outs ordered by the Referee for exceptions (a) and/or (b), the Back Judge shall not sound his whistle until the expiration of extra time is allowed.
(2) The Referee shall sound his whistle for play to start immediately upon Back Judge's signal for the expiration of any team time out.
(3) On all requested time outs, the Referee shall not signify that the ball will be put in play prior to 1 minute and 50 seconds of elapsed time, or 30 seconds during the last two minutes of a half.

Article 5   Prior to the two-minute warning of either half, additional time outs by either team after the third legal one are not allowed unless it is for an injured player who must be immediately designated and removed (except injury time out caused by a foul). An attempt to call an excess time out to "freeze" a kicker prior to a field-goal attempt or a Try attempt is unsportsmanlike conduct. See 12-3-1-v.

After the first three charged time outs during a half, all team time outs, regardless of the reason, are to be counted in determining the fourth or subsequent time outs.

Article 6   Team time outs after two-minute warning of half.

(a) After the two-minute warning of either half, additional time outs by either team after the third legal one are not allowed unless it is for an injured player who must be immediately designated and removed. A fourth time out under these conditions is not penalized. Subsequent requests (fifth or more) under these same conditions are allowed, but are penalized five yards. On all excess time outs against the defense, the play clock is reset to 40 seconds.

Note: An attempt to call an excess time out to "freeze" a kicker prior to a field-goal attempt or a Try attempt is unsportsmanlike conduct. See 12-3-1-v.

(b) After the two-minute warning of either half while time is in, if the score is tied or the team in possession is behind in the score and the offensive team has exhausted its legal time outs, an additional time out may be requested and granted under (a) above. However, the ball shall not be put in play until the time on the game clock has been reduced by 10 seconds. The Referee, in a position between the center and the quarterback, will advise (by using the microphone) the game clock operator to take 10 seconds off the clock. During this time interval, the Umpire will be directly over the ball. After 10 seconds have been taken off the game clock, both officials will back away. After a momentary delay, the Referee will blow his whistle and give the wind-the-clock signal. This signal indicates to the game clock operator to restart the game clock and also to the offensive team that it may legally snap the ball.

Note: There can never be a 10-second run-off against the defensive team.

(c) After the two-minute warning of each half, if there is an excess time out for an injury by either team, time is in with the Referee's whistle for play to start, if the clock had been running. (See 4-3-10 for exceptions).

 Penalty: For each excess time out: Loss of five yards from succeeding spot for delay. Necessary Line and number of down remain the same.

■ Supplemental Notes

(1) Either half can end during the 10-second period between time in and permissible play resumption.

(2) This applies to Sudden Death Rule (Rule 16) in force for Wild Card Playoffs, Divisional Playoffs, Conference Championship Games, the Super Bowl, and the Pro Bowl.

(3) The Rules Committee deprecates feigning injuries, with subsequent withdrawal, to obtain a time out without penalty and even so when done to conserve time. Coaches are urged to cooperate in discouraging this practice. The Referee should refuse such a request when it is an obvious evasion of the rules.

(4) The Referee must notify both captain and head coach when their team has been charged with three time outs, and no penalty is to be enforced for an excess time out unless such notice has been given. The Referee shall not delegate this notification to any other person.

Article 7   Play may be suspended by Referee (Referee's time out)
at any time without penalty to either team when playing
time is being destroyed because of delay not
intentionally caused by either team, provided it does not
violate some specific rule.

■ **Supplemental Notes**

The following situations are automatic Referee's time
outs:

(1) Where there is a change of possession. The game
clock will start on the snap.

(2) Any possibility of a measurement for first down or in
consulting a captain about one.

(3) Any time the player who originally takes the snap is
tackled behind the line of scrimmage. Prior to the
two-minute warning, the Referee will restart the
clock after the ball has been properly spotted.

Exception:

During the last two minutes of a half, the game clock
shall not be stopped after the tackle. The play clock
starts at 40 seconds.

(4) Undue pileups on the runner or ball, or determining
possession after a fumble during time in.

(5) Undue delay by officials in spotting ball for the next
snap.

(6) Illegal recovery of any kicked ball from scrimmage.

(7) The snap made before the officials can assume their
positions (not a repeated act). See 4-3-9-g.

(8) Injury to an official or member of the chain crew.

(9) Captain's choice of a fair catch kick or snap after a
fair catch. See 11-5-3; 10-1-6.

(10) Officials' conference for a rules interpretation or an enforcement (15-1-6). Game clock starts as original status dictates.

(11) Repairing or replacing game equipment (not player equipment).

(12) Line Judge's signal of two-minute warning for a half; the game clock starts on the snap.

(13) Obvious inability of the offense to hear team signals because of crowd noise. When such situations prevail, the following procedures must be followed:

    (a) If the quarterback (or other signal-caller) of the offensive team indicates to the Referee that his teammates cannot hear his signals, and the Referee deems it reasonable to conclude the players on the offense (other than wide receivers) cannot hear, the Referee will extend his right arm fully over his head to indicate disruptive crowd noise. The Referee then will signal a Referee's time out and ask the defensive captain to use his best effort to quiet the crowd. The Referee then will announce over his wireless microphone that he has asked the defensive team to assist in quieting the crowd so that the game can continue. He then will return to his position behind the offensive team.

    (b) If, after the public announcement described in (a) above, crowd noise conditions in that same ball possession are deemed by the Referee, with or without appeal by the offensive signal-caller, to be disruptive to the offense, he again will use the upraised-arm signal and will announce over his wireless microphone that any further crowd noise which is disruptive will result in forfeiture by the defense of one of its remaining time outs in the half or, in the absence of time outs, a five-yard penalty against the defense for delay of the game.

(c) If, after the public announcement described in (b) above, crowd noise conditions in that same ball possession are deemed by the Referee, with or without appeal by the offensive signal-caller, to be disruptive to the offense, he again will use the upraised-arm signal and will, if such signal does not quiet the crowd, assess the appropriate penalty provided for in (b) above.

(d) Thereafter if disruptive crowd noise recurs in the same ball possession, the Referee, with or without appeal from the offensive signal-caller, will use the upraised-arm signal while remaining in his normal position behind the offensive formation and without calling a Referee's time out. Following a momentary pause to confirm that disruptive noise conditions are continuing, he will assess the appropriate penalty provided for in (b) above.

(e) If, upon any appeal from the offensive signal-caller, the Referee deems that noise conditions are not sufficiently disruptive to apply the crowd-noise procedures, he will deny the appeal and proceed with normal game timing. The Referee's signal that he is denying the appeal will be to point toward the defensive team's goal line.

(f) During the time out described in (a) above, the offensive team may huddle. When the offensive team again attempts to run a play, the game clock will start on the snap. The 40/25-second play clock will not be used.

(g) If, in any ball possession subsequent to the first possession of the game that involves disruptive crowd noise, the Referee, either with or without an appeal by the offensive signal-caller, deems it to be reasonable to conclude that the players on offense (other than wide receivers) cannot hear, the Referee will signal a Referee's time out and announce over his wireless microphone that the defensive team is now subject to appropriate crowd-noise penalties. Any crowd-noise interruption thereafter in that same ball possession will result in the Referee using his upraised-arm signal, followed, if necessary, by a penalty against the defense.

(h) Once the procedures of (a) and (b) above have been followed in a given game, disruptive crowd-noise incidents in any subsequent ball possession will be handled by the procedures of (g). In effect, for each ball possession during which disruptive crowd noise occurs (with the exception of the first in the game), the Referee will make one public announcement after which he may assess a penalty, and he will thereafter always precede any such penalty by the upraised-arm signal but not by a public announcement. As specified in (a) and (b) above, he will make two public announcements before assessing a penalty on the first ball possession of the game during which disruptive crowd noise occurs.

(i) In any instance where the Referee is signaling with upraised arm, the offensive signal-caller may, if he chooses, continue to play. Such signal indicates that disruptive crowd-noise conditions prevail; it does not automatically stop play nor does it automatically result in a penalty. Conversely, if the Referee's arm is not upraised, the penalty situation does not prevail and the offense must attempt to continue play.

(14) On a play from scrimmage, if a fumble goes out of bounds forward by any player, the game clock stops on the official's time out signal, then restarts on the wind-of-the-game-clock signal. (See 7-5-6-Note)

(15) On a play not from scrimmage, if a fumble goes out of bounds forward by any player, the game clock stops on the official's time out signal and will restart at the snap.

Article 8 After a Referee's time out, time in starts with his whistle (clock signal).

Exception: After a time out for a change of possession, notification of two minutes remaining for a half, stopping the game clock for inability to hear signals, and after enforcement (when appropriate) time is in with the snap. See 15-1-10.

Article 9 The ball must be put in play promptly and any action or inaction by either team that tends to prevent this is a delay of game. It is delay of game if the ball is not put into play within 40/25 seconds:

(a) by snap after the neutral zone starts (3-18);
(b) after a Referee's time out.

Other examples of action or inaction that are to be construed as delay of game or attempts to conserve playing time are:

(c) Repeatedly charging into the neutral zone prior to the snap when not otherwise ruled encroaching (7-2-3).
(d) With time in, start of neutral zone is unduly delayed by failure of players of either team to assemble promptly.

Note: During last two minutes of half, once the ball has been respotted for the succeeding down and the Head Linesman has placed his bean bag on the ground at the new line of scrimmage, the Umpire, upon signal from the Referee, is to step away from the ball. At this point a snap may be made. If ball is snapped before all members of defensive team have taken their proper position on line of scrimmage, play is to be stopped immediately and that team penalized five yards for offside.

(e) When a player remains on a dead ball or on a runner who has been downed.

(f) Failure to play immediately when ordered, including not kicking the ball on a kickoff, safety kick, or fair-catch kick within the designated 25 seconds on the play clock.

(g) Repeatedly snapping ball after the neutral zone is established before the officials can assume their positions (7-3-3-c-2).

(h) A runner repeatedly attempts to advance after he is so held that his forward progress is stopped, after whistle is blown.

(i) When one of the kickers recovers a kick (unless one recovered behind line other than a Try-kick), and carries it in any direction. See 9-1-4-Note; 9-1-6.

(j) Undue advance by a receiver who catches the ball after a fair catch signal (valid or invalid), unless the ball is first touched by the kickers. See 10-1-2-Exc.

(k) Opponent taking ball from runner after it is dead, causes a loose ball or scramble that consumes playing time to re-spot the ball (7-4-1-d).

(l) Undue delay in assembling after a time out.

(m) Substitute entering during play unless interference (12-3-3).

(n) Defensive player(s) aligned in a stationary position within one yard of the line of scrimmage cannot make quick and abrupt actions that are not part of normal defensive player movement in an obvious attempt to cause an offensive player(s) to foul (false start). (Blow whistle immediately.)

Penalty: For delay of game: Loss of five yards:

(a) from succeeding spot if between downs and ball remains dead; or

(b) from previous spot if ball was in play. Number of down and necessary line remain the same.

Note: After an enforcement for delay of game by the defense, prior to or at the snap, number of down and necessary line remain the same. See 14-8-5.

Article 10 A team is not permitted to conserve time inside of one minute of either half by committing any of the following acts: fouls by either team that prevent the snap (i.e., false start, encroachment, etc.), intentional grounding, an illegal forward pass thrown from beyond the line of scrimmage with the intent to conserve time, throwing a backward pass out of bounds with the intent to conserve time, and any other intentional foul that causes the clock to stop.

Penalty: Loss of five yards unless a larger distance penalty is applicable. When actions referred to above are committed by the offensive team with the clock running, officials will run 10 seconds off the game clock before permitting the ball to be put in play on the ready-for-play signal. The clock will start on the ready-for-play signal. If the offensive team has time outs remaining, it will have the option of using a time

---

out in lieu of a 10-second run-off. If the action is by the defense, the Play Clock will be reset to 40 seconds and the game clock will start on the ready signal. If the defense has time outs remaining, it will have the option of using a time out in lieu of the game clock being started.

Note: There never can be a 10-second run-off against the defensive team.

■ Supplemental Notes

(1) The Play Clock operator shall time the 40/25-second intervals between plays upon signal from game official(s). The 40-second interval is to start when one play ends. If certain administrative stoppages or other delays occur while time is out, such as change of possession, team time out, Referee's time out, injury, measurement, or any unusual delay that interferes with the normal flow of play, the 25-second interval is to be used (even if the 40-second clock was already counting down). The 40/25-second clock is to start when:

   (a) neutral zone starts with Referee's whistle (3-18);

   (b) Referee's whistle indicates that play may start following any time out.

   If the ball is not put in play within this time, he sounds his whistle for the foul and the ball remains dead. When the foul is prior to a snap, defensive team may decline distance penalty, in which case down is replayed. See 14-6-Exc. 4.

(2) If the Play Clock is stopped prior to the snap for any reason while time is in, after the stoppage has concluded, the time remaining on the Play Clock shall be the same as when it stopped, unless:

(a) the stoppage has been for a penalty, a charged team time out, the two-minute warning, or the expiration of a period, in which case the Play Clock shall be reset to 25 seconds; or

(b) fewer than 10 seconds are remaining on the Play Clock, in which case it shall be reset to 10 seconds.

(3) More than two successive penalties, during the same down, after a warning is unsportsmanlike conduct (12-3-1-l, m).

(4) When the ball is dead during time in, the Referee must determine immediately if a measurement is indicated, unless there has been a change of possession. If indicated, he declares a Referee's time out. The distance and downs are to be announced as he assumes his normal stance.

(5) Certain acts of delay may involve stopping the game clock immediately. Repeated violations of substitution rule to conserve time are unsportsmanlike conduct (12-3-1-l and 4-3-9).

(6) During a play from scrimmage a backward pass going out of bounds during the last two minutes of a half stops the game clock. Time is in with the Referee's whistle (clock signal) when the ball is ready for play.

Note: Time for a half can expire before a ball can be put in play following Referee's whistle for play to start.

Article 11 If at the end of any period, time expires while the ball is in play, time is not called until the down ends.

(a) During such a down (i.e., prior to the end of a down): If there is an accepted foul (not one of a double foul) by the defense, the offended team may choose to extend the period by one down (enforcement as usual). If the first or third period is not extended, any penalty (unless declined) is enforced before the start of the succeeding period.

(b) If there is a defensive foul following the end of the second or fourth periods that occurs in the action immediately after the end of a down, the offensive team may choose to extend the period for one untimed down.

(c) If there is a foul by the offense, there shall be no extension of the period. If the foul occurs on the last play of the half, no score made by the offense is counted.

Exception: If the offensive foul is (1) illegal touching of a kick, (2) fair catch interference, (3) palpably unfair act, (4) personal foul or unsportsmanlike foul prior to an interception of a forward pass or the recovery of a backward pass or fumble, or (5) a foul by the kicking team prior to a player of the receiving team securing possession of the ball during a down in which there is a safety kick, a scrimmage kick, or a free kick, the period may be extended by an untimed down, if the defense elects to accept the foul.

(d) If there is a personal foul or unsportsmanlike conduct foul that is (1) not in the continuing action immediately after the end of a down and (2) occurs between the end of the second period and the beginning of the third period (or between the end of the fourth period and the beginning of an overtime period), the penalty shall be enforced on the ensuing kickoff.

(e) If a double foul (14-3) occurs on the last play of the first or third periods, the period is not extended. If a double foul occurs during the last play of either half, extend the period.

Exception: The half is not extended if:

> (1) both fouls are dead ball fouls;
> (2) 5 vs. 15, with major foul on the offense (14-3-1-Exc. 1);
> (3) Double foul with change of possession, clean hands rule (14-3-2).

(f) If a touchdown is made, the Try shall be allowed (except during a sudden-death period).

(g) If a fair catch is signaled and made, receivers may choose to extend the period by one fair-catch-kick down (10-1-6). If the first or third period is not so extended, the receivers may start the succeeding period with a snap or fair catch kick (11-5-3).

(h) If no fair-catch signal is given and the kickers interfere with the receiver's opportunity to catch a kick, the receiving team may extend the period by one down from scrimmage. If a fair catch is signaled and the kickers interfere with the receivers' opportunity to catch a kick, the receiving team may extend the period by either one down from scrimmage or a fair-catch kick (10-1-6).

(i) If the first or third period is extended for any reason, or if a touchdown occurs during the last play of such a period, any additional play, including a Try, shall be completed before change of goal. If a period is extended for any reason, it shall continue until a down free from any foul specified in (a) to (h) is completed.

(j) If a safety occurs during the last play of a half, the score counts. No safety kick is made unless it resulted from a foul, and even so unless receivers request that kick be made.

Article 12 In the last 40 seconds of either half, with the Game Clock running, a defensive foul prior to the snap cannot prevent the termination of a half except for the normal options, including remaining time outs, available to the offensive and defensive team.

Players,
Substitutes,
Equipment

Rule 5

Players, Substitutes, Equipment

Section 1   **PLAYERS**

Article 1   The game is to be played by two teams of 11 players each. If a snap or free kick is made while a team has:

(a) fewer than 11 players on field, ball is in play and there is no penalty;

(b) more than 11 players on field, ball is in play and there is a five-yard penalty (5-2-1); or

(c) a player who fails to inform the Referee of a change of his eligibility when required by rule, no official is to notify team of this fact before play starts and there is a penalty (7-2-4).

Article 2   Each team must designate its captain(s), and that player(s) is the sole representative of his team in all communications with officials. See Rule 18.

Article 3   A captain's first choice from any alternative privileges which may be offered his team, before or during the game, is final and not subject to change.

Article 4   All players must wear numerals on their jerseys in accordance with Rule 5, Section 3, Article 3(c), and such numerals must be by playing position as follows: quarterbacks, punters, and placekickers, 1-19; running backs and defensive backs, 20-49; centers, 50-59 (60-79 if 50-59 unavailable); offensive guards and tackles, 60-79; wide receivers, 10-19 and 80-89; tight ends, 80-89; defensive linemen, 60-79 (90-99 if 60-79 unavailable); and linebackers, 50-59 (90-99 if 50-59 unavailable).

If a player changes his position during his playing career in the NFL and such change moves him out of a category specified above, he must be issued an appropriate new jersey numeral.

Any request to wear a numeral for a special position not specified above (e.g., H-back) must be made to the Commissioner.

During the preseason period when playing rosters are larger, the League will allow duplication and other temporary deviations from the numbering scheme specified above, but the rule must be adhered to for all players during the regular season and postseason. Clubs must make numerals available to adhere to the rule, even if it requires putting back into circulation a numeral that has been retired or withheld for other reasons. See 7-2-4 for reporting change of position.

Article 5   A player must be withdrawn and substituted for when he is disqualified (12-2, 3) or suspended (5-3). A suspended player may re-enter when legal. A disqualified player must leave the playing field enclosure and go to the team locker room within a reasonable time.

Penalties:

(a) **For illegal return: Loss of five yards from succeeding spot after discovery.**

(b) **For return of a disqualified player: Loss of 15 yards and exclusion from playing field enclosure.**

■ Supplemental Notes

(1) Coaches are to assume full responsibility for the legality of substitutions, but this does not preclude a penalty if discovered before or after a substitute reports.

---

(2) If it is not discovered until the end of a down but prior to the start of next one that a player had returned illegally, enforcement is from the previous spot when definitely known. Otherwise, enforcement is from succeeding spot as a foul between downs (14-5).

Section 2   **SUBSTITUTES**

Article 1   Substitutes may not enter the field while the ball is in play. Any entering offensive substitute who participates in a play must enter while the ball is dead and must move onto the field as far as the inside of the field numerals; in addition, the player or players replaced must have cleared the field on their own side (between end lines) prior to the snap or free kick.

There can never be 12 or more players in the offensive huddle.

Note: While in the process of substitution or simulated substitution, the offense is prohibited from rushing quickly to the line and snapping the ball with the obvious attempt to cause a defensive foul; i.e., too many men on the field. If in the judgment of the officials this takes place, the following procedure will be applied:

(1) If the play takes place and a defensive foul results, the flag will be picked up and the down replayed. At this time, the Referee will notify the head coach that any further use of this tactic will result in an unsportsmanlike penalty being assessed.

Note: Covering official(s) will extend both arms horizontally to indicate that substitutions have been made. Also, the same quick-snap rule will not be applicable in the last two minutes of either half.

(2) On a fourth down punting situation, the Referee and the Umpire will not allow a quick snap which would

prevent the defense from having a reasonable time to complete their substitutions. This will apply throughout the entire game.

Penalty: For illegal substitution: Loss of five yards:

(1) **From previous spot if the ball was in play. Number of down and necessary line to gain remains the same:**

    (a) **withdrawn player on field at snap or free-kick; or**

    (b) **clearing field on opponents' side or across end line (whether violation is discovered during down, or at end of down); or**

(2) **From succeeding spot if between downs and ball remains dead:**

    (a) **12-or-more players in huddle (blow whistle immediately).**

Note: Interference with play by illegal substitutes during (a) and (b) is a palpably unfair act (12-3-3).

Interference with play during (a) to (c) is a palpably unfair act (12-3-3).

■ Supplemental Notes

(1) If an illegal substitute enters during a live ball, the penalty will be enforced in accordance to Rule 14.

(2) See 5-1-5 for illegal return or withdrawal.

(3) If a substitute enters during dead ball with time in or after Referee's whistle following a time out, no official is to signal his entry and Back Judge continues his timing of 40/25 seconds, if and when it has been started (4-3-10-S.N. 1).

Exception: On an illegal return, ball remains dead if discovered prior to snap.

(4) Under no circumstances is Referee to delay start of neutral zone because of an incoming substitute.

(5) A substitute is not to report to an official. He becomes a player when:

　a) he informs a teammate that he is replacing him;

　b) he participates in at least one play after communicating with a teammate;

　c) a teammate voluntarily withdraws upon his entering; or

　d) in the absence of any of the above a, b, or c, he is on the field at snap, fair-catch kick, or free kick, or when a snap, fair-catch kick, or free kick is imminent.

(6) A player is legally in the game when he has participated in at least one play.

(7) A player is legally substituted for when he leaves the game for at least one play.

(8) A substitute may not enter the field of play, proceed to the area of the huddle, communicate with a teammate(s), and then leave the field without participating in one play. Violations of this rule will be penalized as Unsportsmanlike Conduct. (12-3-1-h)

(9) Referee shall sound his whistle for play to start immediately upon completion of a penalty for an illegal substitution, return, or withdrawal. The game clock will start as appropriate. See 4-3-10.

Article 2　　After the two-minute warning of either half, a violation of the substitution rule occurs while ball is dead with time in by the team in possession.

(a) If the act is designed to conserve time, Referee stops play, penalizes, and will run off 10 seconds prior to allowing ball to be put in play. Clock starts when

Umpire lowers his arm and gives wind-the-game-clock signal. See 4-3-10.

(b) Repeated violations of substitution rule to conserve time are unsportsmanlike conduct (12-3-1-m).

Section 3   **EQUIPMENT, UNIFORMS, PLAYER APPEARANCE**

Article 1   Throughout the game-day period while in view of the stadium and television audience, including during pregame warm-ups, all players must dress in a professional manner under the uniform standards specified in this Section 3. They must wear equipment offering reasonable protection to themselves while reasonably avoiding risk of injury to other players. And they generally must present an appearance that is appropriate to representing their individual clubs and the National Football League. The term uniform, as used in this policy, applies to every piece of equipment worn by a player, including helmet, shoulder pads, thigh pads, knee pads, and any other item of protective gear, and to every visible item of apparel, including but not limited to pants, jerseys, wristbands, gloves, stockings, shoes, visible undergarments, and accessories such as headwear coverings worn under helmets and hand towels. All visible items worn on game-day by players must be issued by the club or the League, or, if from outside sources, must have approval in advance by the League office.

Article 2   Pursuant to the official colors established for each NFL club in the League Constitution and Bylaws, playing squads are permitted to wear only those colors or a combination of those colors for helmets, jerseys, pants, and stockings; provided that white is also an available color for jerseys and mandatory color for the lower portion of stockings [see 5-3-3-f, "Stockings," below]. Each player on a given team must wear the same colors on his uniform as all other players on his team in the same game. Before July 1 each year, home clubs are required to report to the League office their choice of jersey color (either white or official team color) for their home games of that forthcoming season (including postseason, in the event that the club should become a host for such a game), and visiting clubs must wear the opposite. For preseason, regular season, or postseason games, the two competing teams may wear jerseys in their official colors (non-white), provided the Commissioner determines that such colors are of sufficient contrast.

Article 3   All players must wear the equipment and uniform apparel listed below, which must be of a suitably protective nature, must be designed and produced by a professional manufacturer, and must not be cut, reduced in size, or otherwise altered unless for medical reasons approved in advance by the Commissioner; provided, however, that during pregame warm-ups players may omit certain protective equipment at their option, except that helmets must be worn. Where additional rules are applicable to specific categories of mandatory equipment or apparel, or where related equipment is optional, such provisions are also spelled out below.

(a) Helmet with chin strap (white only) fastened and face mask attached. Face masks must not be more than 5/8-inch in diameter and must be made of rounded material; transparent materials are prohibited.

Clear (transparent) plastic face shields for eye protection are optional. Tinted eye shields may be worn only after the League office is supplied with appropriate medical documentation and approval is subsequently granted. The League office has final approval. League office is supplied in advance with appropriate medical documentation that the shield is needed.

No visible identification of a manufacturer's name or logo on the exterior of a helmet or on any attachment to a helmet is permitted unless provided for under a commercial arrangement between the League and manufacturer; in no event is identification of any helmet manufacturer permitted on the visible surface of a rear cervical pad. All helmets must carry a small NFL shield logo on the rear lower-left exterior, which logo will be provided in quantity by the League. All helmets must carry on the rear lower right exterior, an approved warning label (such labels will be supplied in quantity by the League).

(b) Jersey must cover all pads and other protective equipment worn on the torso and upper arms, and must be appropriately tailored to remain tucked into the uniform pants throughout the game. Tearaway jerseys are prohibited. Mesh jerseys with large fish-net material (commonly referred to as "bullet-hole" or "port-hole" mesh) are also prohibited. Surnames of players in letters a minimum of 2½ inches high must be affixed to the exterior of jerseys across the upper back above the numerals; nicknames are prohibited; and in cases of duplicate surnames, the first initial of the given name must be used. All jerseys must carry a small NFL Equipment logo at the middle of the yoke of the neck on the front of the garment. All fabrics must be approved by the League office prior to production.

(c) Numerals on the back and front of jerseys in accordance with Rule 5, Section 1, Article 4. Such numerals must be a minimum of 8 inches high and 4 inches wide, and their color must be in sharp contrast with the color of the jersey. Smaller numerals should be worn on the tops of the shoulders or upper arms of the jersey. Small numerals on the back of the helmet or on the uniform pants are optional.

(d) Pants must be worn over the entire knee area; pants shortened or rolled up to meet the stockings above the knee are prohibited. No part of the pants may be cut away unless an appropriate gusset or other device is used to replace the removed material. All pants must carry a small NFL Equipment logo on the front left groin area of the pants, midway between the fly opening and side seam, and ½-inch below the belt.

(e) Shoulder pads must be completely covered by the uniform jersey.

(f) Stockings must cover the entire area from the shoe to the bottom of the pants, and must meet the pants below the knee. Players are permitted to wear as many layers of stockings and tape on the lower leg as they prefer, provided the exterior is a one-piece stocking that includes solid white from the top of the shoe to the midpoint of the lower leg, and approved team color or colors (non-white) from that point to the top of the stocking. Uniform stockings may not be altered (e.g. over-stretched, or cut at the toes, or sewn short) in order to bring the line between solid white and team colors lower or higher than the mid-point of the lower leg. No other stockings and/or opaque tape may be worn over the one-piece, two-color uniform stocking. Barefoot punters and placekickers may omit the stocking of the kicking foot in preparation for and during kicking plays.

(g) Shoes must be of standard football design, including "sneaker" type shoes such as basketball shoes, cross-training shoes, etc. League-approved tricolored shoes are permitted with black, white, and one team color. Each team must select a dominant color for its shoes, either black or white (with a conforming selection of either all-black or all-white shoelaces). The selection of dominant color must be reported by each team to the League office no later than July 1 each year. Each player may select among shoe styles previously approved by the League office. All players on the same team must wear shoes with the same dominant color. Approved shoe syles will contain one team color which must be the same for all players on a given team. A player may wear an unapproved standard football shoe style as long as the player tapes over the entire shoe to conform to his team's selected dominant color. Logos, names, or other commercial identification on shoes are not permitted to be visible unless advance approval is granted by the League office (see Article 7). Size and location of logos and names on shoes must be approved by the NFL. When a shoe logo or a name approved by the League office is covered with an appropriate use of tape (see 5-4-f), players will be allowed to cut out the tape covering the original logo or name, provided the cut is clean and is the exact size of the logo or name. The logo or name of the shoe manufacturer must not be re-applied to the exterior of taped shoes unless advance approval is granted by the League office. Kicking shoes must not be modified (including using a shoelace wrapped around toe and/or bottom of the shoe), and any shoe that is worn by a player with an artificial limb on his kicking leg must have a kicking surface that conforms to that of a normal kicking shoe. Punters and placekickers may omit the shoe from the kicking foot in preparation for and during kicking plays. Punters and placekickers may wear any combination of tri-colored shoes provided that the colors are consistent with those selected by the team and with the policy listed above.

Article 4 In addition to the several prohibited items of equipment and apparel specified in Article 3 above, the following are also prohibited:

(a) Metal or other hard objects that project from a player's person or uniform, including from his shoes.

(b) Hard objects and substances, including but not limited to casts, guards, or braces for hand, wrist, forearm, elbow, hip, thigh, knee, shin, unless such items are appropriately covered on all edges and surfaces by a minimum of ⅜-inch foam rubber or similar soft material. Any such item worn to protect an injury must be reported by the applicable coaching staff to the Umpire in advance of the game, and a description of the injury must be provided. If the Umpire determines that an item in question, including tape or bandages on hands or forearms, may present undue risk to other players, he may prevent its use at a time before or during a game until the item is removed or appropriately corrected.

(c) Detachable kicking toe.

(d) Torn or improperly fitting equipment creating a risk of injury to other players, e.g. the hard surfaces of shoulder pads exposed by a damaged jersey.

(e) Shoe cleats made of aluminum or other material that may chip, fracture, or develop a cutting edge. Conical cleats with concave sides or points which measure less than ⅜-inch in diameter at the tips, or cleats with oblong ends which measure less than ¼- by ¾-inch at the end tips are also prohibited. Nylon cleats with flat steel tips are permitted.

(f) Opaque, contrasting-color tape that covers any part of the helmet, jersey, pants, stockings, or shoes; transparent tape or tape of the same color as the background material is permissible for use on these items of apparel. Players may use opaque white tape on hands and arms, provided it conforms to 5-3-4(b) above ("Uncovered Hard Objects, Substances") and 5-3-4(h) below ("Approved Glove Color on Linemen"). Opaque tape on shoes is permitted, provided it is the same color as the shoe, and provided it does not carry up into the stocking area.

(g) Headgear or any other equipment or apparel which, in the opinion of the Referee, may confuse an opponent because of its similarity in color to that of the game football. If such color is worn, it must be broken by stripes or other patterns of sharply contrasting color or colors.

(h) Gloves, wrappings, elbow pads, and other items worn on the arms below or over the jersey sleeves by interior offensive linemen (excluding tight ends) which are of a color different from that which is mandatorily reported to the League office by the club before July 1 each year. Such reported color must be white or other official color of the applicable team, and, once reported, must not be changed throughout that same season. Players at other positions (non-interior linemen) also may wear gloves provided they are a solid white, solid black, or a solid color that is an official color of the applicable club. Gloves may also be a tri-color combination of black, white, and one (1) official color of the applicable club. Gloves may also be a bi-color combination of black or white with one (1) official color of the applicable team. Clubs are not required to designate to the League office by July 1, the color of gloves that will be worn by their non-interior linemen.

(i) Adhesive or slippery substances on the body, equipment, or uniform of any player; provided, however, that players may wear gloves with a tackified surface if such tacky substance does not adhere to the football or otherwise cause handling problems for players.

(j) Quarterbacks will be allowed to wear under the game jersey a solid color T-shirt, turtleneck, or sweatshirt (consistent with team undergarment color) with sleeves cut to any length, as long as both sleeves are evenly trimmed and the edges are sewn and hemmed. All other players may wear garments under game jerseys only if the undergarment sleeves either (a) do not extend below the sleeves of the jersey; or (b) are full length to the wrist. No other sleeve lengths for garments under jerseys are permitted for players other than quarterbacks. Players may not wear long-sleeved undergarments that include pebble-grip sleeves. Any garments under jerseys that are exposed at the neck or sleeve area and that carry an exposed logo or commercial name must be licensed by and approved by the League office for wear on the field (see Article 7). All members of the same team who wear approved undergarments with exposed necks or sleeves must wear the same color on a given day, which color must be white or a solid color that is an official team color (solid means that sleeves must not carry stripes, designs, or team names).

(k) Players are not permitted to wear bandannas, stockings, or other unapproved headwear anywhere on the field during the pregame, game, or postgame periods, even if such items are worn under their helmet.

Article 5   It is recommended that all players wear hip pads, thigh pads, and knee pads which reasonably avoid the risk of injury. Unless otherwise provided by individual team policy, it is the players' responsibility and decision whether to follow this recommendation and use such pads. If worn, all three forms of pads listed above must be covered by the outer uniform. Basketball-type knee pads are permitted but must also be covered by the outer uniform.

Article 6   Among the types of optional equipment that are permitted to be worn by players are the following:

(a) Rib protectors ("flak jackets") under the jersey.

(b) Wristbands, provided they are white or black only.

(c) Towels, provided they are white licensed towels approved by the League office for use on the playing field. Players are prohibited from adding to these towels personal messages, logos, names, symbols, or illustrations. Such towels also must be attached to or tucked into the front waist of the pants, and must be no larger than 6 x 8 inches (slightly larger size may be issued to quarterbacks, or may be folded to these limits for wearing in games). A player may wear no more than one towel. Players are prohibited from discarding on the playing field any loose towels or other materials used for wiping hands and the football. Streamers or ribbons, regardless of length, hanging from any part of the uniform, including the helmet, are prohibited.

(d) When players are on the field, as defined in Article 1, during the pregame, game and postgame periods, they may wear approved caps, approved cold-weather gear, or other approved headwear coverings for medical purposes only, as determined by the Commissioner. Any permissible head coverings must be approved by the League office, and if worn under the helmet, no portion may hang from or otherwise be visible outside the helmet.

Article 7   Throughout the period on game-day that a player is visible to the stadium and television audience (including in pregame warm-ups, in the bench area, and during postgame interviews in the locker room or on the field), players are prohibited from wearing, displaying, or orally promoting equipment, apparel, or other items that carry commercial names or logos of companies, unless such commercial identification has been approved in advance by the League office. The size of any approved logo or other commercial identification involved in an agreement between a manufacturer and the League will be modest and unobtrusive, and there is no assurance that it will be visible to the television audience. Subject to any future approved arrangements with a manufacturer and subject to any decision by the Commissioner to suspend enforcement temporarily of this provision governing shoes, visible logos, and names of shoes are prohibited, including on the sole of the shoe that may be seen from time to time during the game.

Article 8   Throughout the period on game-day that a player is visible to the stadium and television audience (including in pregame warm-ups, in the bench area, and during postgame interviews in the locker room or on the field), players are prohibited from wearing, displaying, or otherwise conveying personal messages either in writing or illustration, unless such message has been approved in advance by the League office. Items to celebrate anniversaries or memorable events, or to honor or commemorate individuals, such as helmet decals, arm bands, and jersey patches on players' uniforms, are prohibited unless approved in advance by the League office. All such items must relate to team or League events or personages. The League will not grant permission for any club or player to wear, display, or otherwise convey messages, through helmet decals, arm bands, jersey patches, or other items affixed to game uniforms or equipment, which relate to political activities or causes, other non-football events, causes or campaigns, or charitable causes or campaigns.

Further, such armbands and jersey patches must be modest in size, tasteful, non-commercial, and non-controversial; must not be worn for more than one football season; and if approved for use by a specific team, must not be worn by players on other teams in the League.

Article 9 Consistent with the equipment and uniform rules of this Section 3, players must otherwise present a professional and appropriate appearance while before the public on game-day. Among the types of activity that are prohibited are use of tobacco products (smokeless included) while in the bench area and use of facial makeup. The Referee is authorized to use his judgment in determining whether any other unusual appearance or behavior is in violation of this Article 9.

Penalties:

(a) For violation of this Section 3 discovered during pregame warmups or at other times prior to the game, player will be advised to make appropriate correction; if violation is not corrected, player will not be permitted to enter the game.

(b) For violation of this Section 3 discovered while player is in game, player will be advised to make appropriate correction at the next change of possession; if violation is not corrected, player will not be permitted to enter the game. Provided, however, if the violation involves the competitive aspects of the game (e.g. illegal kicking toe of shoe, an adhesive or slippery substance) player will be suspended immediately upon discovery.

(c) For repeat violation: disqualification from game.

(d) For illegal entry or return of a player suspended under this Section 3: loss of 5 yards from succeeding spot and removal until properly equipped after one down.

(e) For violation of this Section 3 detected in the bench area: player and head coach will be asked to remove the objectionable item, properly equip the player, or otherwise correct the violation. The involved player or players will be disqualified from the game if correction is not made promptly.

■ Supplemental Notes

Note 1: In addition to the game-day penalties specified above, the Commissioner may subsequently impose independent disciplinary action on the involved player, up to and including suspension from the team's next succeeding game—preseason, regular season, or postseason, whichever is applicable.

Note 2: If a player is suspended for having adhesive or slippery substances on his body, equipment, or uniform, he must remain out of the game for one play, independent if there is a team time out, the two-minute warning, or the end of a period.

Note 3: If a player (kicker) is suspended for having an illegal kicking shoe, he must remain out of the game for one play, unless there is a team time out, the two-minute warning, or the end of the period.

Free Kick

Rule 6

Free Kick

Section 1   **PUTTING BALL IN PLAY**

Article 1   A free kick called a kickoff (3-16) puts the ball in play:

(a) at the start of each half;

(b) after a Try; and

(c) after a successful field goal.

Article 2   A free kick also puts the ball in play:

(a) after a safety (see 3-12-1b);

(b) when there is a replay for a short free kick (6-2-1); and

(c) when enforcement for a foul during a free kick is from the previous spot (6-2-5).

Note: The ball is put in play by a snap in all other cases (7-3-1).

Article 3   A free kick may be made from any point on or behind the offensive team's free-kick line and between inbounds lines. A dropkick, placekick, or punt may be used.

Exceptions:

1) A punt may not be used on a kickoff.

2) During a placekick at the kickoff, the kicking team may use a manufactured tee that is 1-inch in height and approved by the League. Once the ball has been placed on the kicking tee, the kicking tee cannot be moved. If this action occurs, the covering officials must stop play and restart the timing process without penalty to the kicking team.

Note: When the mark of a fair catch is in a side zone, it is considered to be on the inbounds line.

Penalty: For illegal kick at free kick: Loss of five yards from previous spot.

Article 4   The initial free-kick lines during a given free kick shall be as follows (plus or minus any distance they might be moved because of a distance penalty enforced prior to the kick):

For the kicking team:

(a) Kickoff—offensive 30
(b) Safety kick—offensive 20

For the receiving team:

A yard line 10 yards in advance of the offensive team's free-kick line.

Note: Kicking team's final free-kick line is a yard line through the spot of the ball when kicked.

Article 5   After the Referee's whistle prior to a free kick:

(a) All receiving players (Team B) must be inbounds and behind their line until the ball is kicked.
(b) All kicking players (Team A) must be inbounds and behind the ball when kicked except the holder of the placekick (3-23) may be beyond the line, and the kicker may be beyond the line but his kicking foot may not be. At least four Team A players must be on each side of the kicker when the ball is kicked.

Penalties:

(a) **For violation of free-kick formation: Loss of 5 yards from previous spot or the succeeding spot.**
(b) **For kicking team offside: Loss of 5 yards from the previous spot or the succeeding spot.**

Section 2   BALL IN PLAY AFTER FREE KICK

Article 1   A free kick is short when it does not go to or across the receiving team's free-kick line unless, before doing so, it is first touched by a player of the receiving team, or goes out of bounds. See 11-5-3-Exc.

Penalties:

(a) **For the first short free kick: Loss of five yards from the previous spot, and rekick must be made.**

Exception: There will not be a rekick inside the last five minutes of the second half.

Note: If there are multiple fouls by the kicking team during a short free-kick, the receiving team can accept the distance penalty that is the most advantageous. This is still to be considered the first short free-kick.

(b) **For the second (or more) consecutive short free-kick illegally touched: The receiving team takes possession of the ball at the spot of illegal touch or recovery. If a re-kick is to be made, new free-kick lines are set. See 6-3-1-b.**

Article 2   Free-Kick Recovery

(a) If a free kick is recovered by the receiving team it may advance.

(b) If a free kick (legal or illegal) is recovered by the kicking team, the ball is dead. If the recovery is legal, the kicking team next puts the ball in play at the spot of recovery. Undue advance by the kicking team recovering (legal or illegal) is delay of game (4-3-9).

(c) If a free kick is simultaneously recovered by two opposing players, the ball is awarded to the receiving team.

Article 3   All general rules apply when play continues after a free
kick (loose ball) ends.

Article 4   No player of the kicking team may touch or recover a
kickoff or safety kick before:

(a) it is touched by the receiving team (B) if that kicking
team player has been out of bounds during the kick;
or

(b) it has crossed the receiving team's restraining line,
unless before doing so it has first been touched by
the receiving team.

**Penalty: For illegal touching of a free kick by the
kicking team: Loss of five yards from the previous spot.
New free-kick lines are set if enforced.**

Article 5   If there is a foul other than a personal foul (blocking)
after a fair-catch signal, fair-catch interference, or an
invalid fair-catch signal during a free kick, any enforcement, if made, is from the previous spot and the free
kick must be made again (10-1-3; 10-1-4; and 10-1-1).

<u>**Exception:**</u> <u>If a foul by the kicking team occurs during a
free-kick play prior to a player of the receiving team
securing possession of the ball, the offended team will
have the option of taking the penalty at the previous
spot and replaying the down or adding the penalty
yardage on to the end of the play.</u>

■ Supplemental Notes

(1) After the ball touches a receiving-team player, any
player may use his hands or arms on an opponent
in an actual legal attempt to recover the ball
(12-1-2-b).

(2) A kicking-team player may not block or use his
hands or arms on an opponent within the first 10

yards, if the ball has not gone 10 yards. This is a 10-yard penalty.

(3) If the ball has not gone beyond 10 yards, a kicking-team player may block or use his hands or arms on an opponent beyond the first 10 yards.

(4) If the ball has gone beyond 10 yards, a kicking team player may block or use his hands on an opponent within the first 10 yards.

(5) Running into the kicker by the receiving team before he recovers his balance is a 5-yard penalty.

Section 3   FREE KICK OUT OF BOUNDS OR IN TOUCH

Article 1 The kicking team may not kick a free kick out of bounds between the goal lines.

Exception: If the receiving team is the last one to touch the kick before it goes out of bounds, it is not a foul by the kicking team, and the receiving team next puts the ball in play at the inbounds spot.

Penalties:

(a) **Receivers' ball 30 yards from the spot of the kick, or the receivers may elect to take possession of the ball at the out-of-pocket spot.**

Exception: If the ball, without going 20 yards, goes out of bounds the first time an onside kick is attempted, the kicking team is to be penalized five yards and a rekick must be made (no declinations), except inside the last five minutes of the second half when there will not be a rekick. While the receiving team may not waive the kicking team's obligations to rekick, it is not deprived of a choice of distance penalties in case of a multiple foul.

(b) **For the second (or more) consecutive onside kick out of bounds, or for any onside kick out of bounds**

inside the last five minutes of the second half:
Receiving team takes possession of the ball at the
out-of-bounds spot.

Article 2   Rule 11 governs if a free kick:

(a) goes out of bounds behind the receiving team's goal
     line;

(b) kickoff or safety kick becomes dead because the ball
     strikes the receiving team's goal post; or

(c) is downed in the end zone.

Scrimmage

Rule 7

Scrimmage

Section 1   **NECESSARY GAIN ON DOWNS**

Article 1   A new series (first-and-10) is awarded to the offensive
team when the following conditions exist; subject,
however, to the specific rules of enforcement (Rule 12).

(a) When, during a given series, the ball is declared dead
in possession of offensive team while it is on, above,
or across the necessary line, or unless a penalty places
it there, or unless a touchback for them results.

(b) When the ball is dead in the field of play in the
offense's possession, after having been in the defensive team's possession during the same down.

(c) When a foul is made by the defense, except as otherwise specified (14-8-5), or when an impetus by them
results in a touchback for offensive team.

(d) When the kicking team recovers a scrimmage kick
anywhere in the field of play after it first has been
touched beyond the line by the receivers. See 9-1-6-
Note.

Article 2   The *forward part of the ball* in its position when declared
dead in the field of play shall be taken as the determining point in measuring any distance gained. *The ball
shall not be rotated when measuring.*

*Note: A ball in the end zone which is carried toward the
field of play is still in touch. It is a safety or touchback if
any part of the ball is on, above, or behind the goal line
(plane) when dead. In such a case, the ball must be entirely
in the field of play in order not to be in touch.*

Article 3   If offensive team fails to advance ball to necessary line
during a given series, it is awarded to defensive team for
a new series at the spot:

(a) where dead at end of fourth down; or

(b) where it is placed because of a combination penalty (14-8-2) or a touchback for defensive team.

Exceptions: Ball is not awarded to defensive team when fourth down results either in:

(a) a safety by the offensive team; or

(b) a touchback for the offensive team.

Section 2	**POSITION OF PLAYERS AT SNAP**

Article 1   The offensive team must have:

(a) seven or more players on its line (3-17) at the snap.

(b) all players who are not on line, other than the snap receiver under center, must be at least one yard behind it at snap, except as provided in 7-2-4.

Note: Offensive linemen may lock legs.

Article 2   <u>During a field-goal attempt or a Try, a Team B player, who is within one yard of the line of scrimmage at the snap, must have his helmet outside the snapper's shoulder pads.</u>

<u>**Penalty: For illegal formation by the defense: Loss of five yards from previous spot.**</u>

Article 3   After the neutral zone starts, no player of either team at snap may:

(a) encroach upon it (3-18); or

(b) be offside (3-19).

Note 1: It is a Neutral-Zone Infraction when a defender moves beyond the neutral zone prior to the snap and is parallel to or beyond an offensive lineman, with an unabated path to the quarterback or kicker. Even though no contact is made by a blocker; officials are to blow their whistles immediately.

> *Note 2: It is a Neutral-Zone Infraction when a defender enters the neutral zone prior to the snap, causing the offensive player(s) in close proximity to react (move) immediately; officials are to blow their whistles immediately. If there is no immediate reaction by the offensive player(s) in close proximity, and the defensive player returns to a legal position prior to the snap without contacting an opponent, there is no foul. For offensive linemen aligned from tight end to tight end, a player is in close proximity if he is within 2½ players of another player. For flexed or split receivers, a player is in close proximity if he is anywhere between the flexed or split receiver and the ball.*

Penalty: For encroachment, offside, or a Neutral-Zone Infraction: Loss of five yards from previous spot. Number of down and necessary line remain the same.

■ Supplemental Notes

> (1) If any player crosses his line and contacts an opponent, it is encroaching. Blow whistle immediately on contact.
>
> (2) If a defensive player charges into the neutral zone, and the action draws an immediate reaction by an offensive player in close proximity, the action by the defense is a Neutral-Zone Infraction.
>
> (3) If a player charges into neutral zone without violating items (2) and (3), and returns to a legal position prior to the snap, it is not encroaching unless it is a repeated act after a warning.

Article 4 An offensive player who comes into game wearing an illegal number for the position he takes must report to the Referee who in turn will report same to the defensive captain. The clock shall not be stopped and the ball may not be put in play until the Referee takes his normal position.

Penalties:

a) **Five yards for illegal substitution if player in above category enters the game and/or his team's huddle without reporting and later reports his player position status to the Referee prior to snap.**

b) **For failure to notify Referee of change in eligibility or ineligibility status (when required) prior to snap: Loss of five yards for illegal substitution.**

■ Supplemental Notes

(1) It is not necessary for entering substitutes or players legally in the game to report to the Referee under the following conditions:

a)   players wearing eligible pass-receiver numbers playing in eligible pass-receiver positions; or

b)   players wearing ineligible pass-receiver numbers playing in ineligible pass-receiver positions.

(2) When a player is legally designated (Referee informed) as being eligible or ineligible (Article 3), he must participate in such a position until legally withdrawn. If the player remains in this position, he must report on every play.

Exception: If the change in playing position status is followed by: 1) a touchdown; 2) a completed kick from scrimmage (a punt, drop kick, or place kick); 3) a foul; 4) a team time out; 5) the end of a quarter; 6) time out for the two-minute warning; 7) a replay challenge; or 8) change of possession, the said player may return to his originally eligible or ineligible playing position without restriction. However, if the kick is not completed or a touchdown not made, the said player must remain in his new position until legally withdrawn for one down (5-1-5). If withdrawn, he is to re-enter to the position indicated by his number unless he again informs the Referee that he is assuming a position other than that designated by his number.

(3) Coaches must instruct those players wearing numbers not qualifying them for designated positions to report to the Referee, prior to the huddle, their change in eligibility or ineligibility status. This rule prevails whether player is already in the game or is an entering substitute and whether it is a play from scrimmage; an attempted field goal; or a Try after touchdown.

(4) The Referee especially must be alert to the above situation at all times and be certain that the defensive captain is notified of the change of any player position status.

Article 5   At the snap, a center, guard, or tackle of the offensive team may be anywhere on his line, but he may not be behind it unless he is at least one yard behind it and has informed the Referee of his change of position to that of an eligible receiver (7-2-4).

Penalty: For center, guard, or tackle not on the line at the snap: Loss of five yards from the previous spot.

Article 6   At the snap, all offensive players must be stationary in their positions:

(a) without any movement of feet, head, or arms;

(b) without swaying of body; and

(c) without moving directly forward except that one player only and he, playing in a backfield position, may be in motion provided he is moving, parallel to, obliquely backward from, or directly backward from the line of scrimmage at snap.

Note 1: No player is ever permitted to be moving obliquely or directly forward toward his opponent's goal line at snap.

Note 2: Non-abrupt movement of head and/or shoulders by offensive players prior to the snap is legal. Players must come to a stop before ball is snapped. If officials judge the action of the offensive players to be abrupt, false start foul is to be called.

Penalty: For player illegally in motion at snap: Loss of five yards from previous spot. In case of doubt, this penalty shall be enforced.

Article 7   After a shift or huddle all offensive players after assuming a set position must come to an absolute stop. They also must remain stationary in their position without any movement of their feet, head, or arms, or swaying of their body for a period of at least one second before snap.

Penalty: For illegal pause or motion after a shift: Loss of five yards from previous spot. In case of doubt the penalty is to be enforced.

■ Supplemental Notes

(1) A single man in motion is not a shift, but if he is moving directly forward at the snap, it is illegal motion (7-2-6-c).

(2) After a shift if all players come to a legal stop and then one or more men start again before snap, the play may result in encroaching (7-2-3), illegal motion (7-2-6), a second shift (7-2-7), or a false start (7-3-4).

Article 8   No player may be out of bounds at the snap.

Penalty: For player out of bounds at snap: Loss of five yards from the previous spot.

Section 3   PUTTING THE BALL IN PLAY

Article 1   The offensive team must put the ball in play with a snap at the spot where the previous down ended, unless the down ended outside the inbounds lines, at which time

---

the ball is put in play by a snap at the nearest inbounds line. If a fair-catch kick is chosen after a fair catch, 10-1-6 and 11-5-3 apply.

Penalty: For not using a snap when prescribed: Loss of five yards.

Article 2   When a foul occurs, the ball shall not be put in play again until the penalty has been (Rule 14):

(a) enforced;
(b) declined;
(c) offset;
(d) annulled by a choice; or
(e) disregarded.

Article 3   The snap (3-31) may be made by any offensive player who is on the line but must conform to the following provisions:

(a) The snap must start with ball on ground with its long axis horizontal and at right angles to line, and

(b) The impulse must be given by one quick and continuous motion of hand or hands of snapper. The ball must actually leave or be taken from his hands during this motion.

(c) The snapper may not:

(1) move his feet abruptly from the start of snap until the ball has left his hands;

(2) have quick plays after the neutral zone starts if the officials have not had a reasonable time to assume their normal stances.

Penalty: For illegally snapping ball: Loss of five yards from spot of snap for false start.

Article 4   From the start of the neutral zone until the snap, no offensive player, if he assumed a set position, shall charge or move in such a way as to simulate the start of a play (false start).

Penalty: For false start: Loss of five yards from previous spot.

■ **Supplemental Notes**

(1) When interior lineman of the offensive team (tackle to tackle) takes or simulates a three-point stance and then moves after taking that stance, the offensive team shall be penalized for a false start. The official *must* blow his whistle immediately.

(2) The penalty for a false start (Article 4) shall be enforced regardless of whether snap is made. The distance penalty for the false start may be declined.

(3) Any quick, abrupt movement by a single offensive player or by several offensive players in unison, which simulates the start of the snap is a false start.

Exception: This does not apply to an offensive player under the center who turns his head or shoulders (only) provided he receives a hand-to-hand snap. Any obvious attempt by the quarterback to draw an opponent offside is a false-start penalty.

(4) Any extension of hands by a player under center as if to receive the snap is a false start unless, while under center, he receives the snap. This includes any player under or behind the center placing his hands on his knees or on the body of the center. It is legal for a player under center who has extended his hands to legally go in motion. If the action draws an immediate reaction from opponent(s), who is in close proximity, it is a false start. If a quarterback goes in motion, he must come to a complete stop prior to the ball being snapped.

(5) Any offensive backfield player, not under center, including a kicker or a place-kick holder who extends his hands, does not have to receive the snap, nor must he retract them prior to the snap.

Article 5   Prior to the snap no defensive player shall enter the neutral zone and touch the ball.

Penalty: For actions interfering with the ball prior to or during the snap: Loss of five yards for delay from the previous spot. Blow whistle immediately on contact.

Article 6   The snap must be to a player who was not on his line at the snap, unless it has first struck the ground. The play continues as after any other backward pass (8-4-4-Exc.) if the snap either:

(a) first touches the ground; or
(b) first touched or is caught by an eligible backfield receiver.

Penalty: For snapping to ineligible snap receiver: Blow whistle. Loss of five yards from the previous spot.

Article 7   Ball is next put in play (snap) at inbounds spot by the team entitled to possession (7-1-1 and 7-1-3; and 7-3-1) when:

(a) a loose ball is out of bounds between goal lines;
(b) a runner is out of bounds between goal lines;
(c) the ball is dead in a side zone;
(d) the ball is placed there as the result of an enforcement; or
(e) the mark of a fair catch is in a side zone (6-1-3-Note).

Exceptions: The ball is next put in play at the previous spot if:

(a) a forward pass goes out of bounds;
(b) a forward pass falls incomplete; or

(c) a foul by the defense occurs in a side zone during an unsuccessful Try.

Section 4   **DEAD BALL**

Article 1   An official shall declare dead ball and the down ended:

(a) when a runner is out of bounds or declares himself down by falling to the ground and makes no effort to advance.

(b) any time a quarterback immediately drops to his knee (or simulates dropping his knee to the ground) behind the line of scrimmage during the last two minutes of a half. The game clock will not stop during this action.

(c) whenever a runner declares himself down by sliding feet first on the ground. The ball is dead at the spot of the ball at the instant the runner so touches the ground.

(d) when a runner is so held or otherwise restrained that his forward progress ends.

(e) when a runner is contacted by a defensive player and he touches the ground with any part of his body except his hands or feet, ball shall be declared dead immediately.

Note: The ball is dead at the spot of the ball at the instant the runner so touches the ground, irrespective of the condition of the field. A runner touching the ground with his hands or feet while in the grasp of an opponent may continue to advance.

(f) when an opponent takes a ball (hand in hand) in possession of a runner who is down on the ground.

(g) when any forward pass (legal or illegal) is incomplete (8-1-5).

(h) when any legal kick touches receivers' goal posts or crossbar unless it later scores a goal from field (9-1-14).

(i) when any scrimmage kick that has not been touched by a player of the receiving team crosses the receiver's goal line from the impetus of the kick and no attempt is made to run it out, or when it touches the ground or a player of the kicking team.

(j) when any legal kick or a short free-kick is recovered by the kickers, except one kicked from behind line which is recovered behind line (not a Try-kick). See 9-1-4-Note for exception.

(k) when defense gains possession during a Try, or a Try-kick ceases to be in play.

(l) when a touchdown, touchback, safety, field goal, or Try has been made.

(m) when any receiver catches or recovers the ball after a fair-catch signal (valid or invalid) before kick is touched by an opponent.

(n) when any official sounds his whistle, even though inadvertently.

(o) when any fourth-down fumble by offensive team is recovered or caught by any offensive player other than the fumbling player. See 8-4-2-Exc. and S.N.

(p) when the ball is out of bounds.

Note: An opponent may take or grab a ball (hand to hand) in possession of a runner provided the runner is on his feet or is airborne.

Article 2   If a loose ball comes to rest anywhere in field and no player attempts to recover, official covering the play should pause momentarily before signaling dead ball (official's time out). Any legal kick is awarded to receivers and any other ball to team last in possession. When awarded to a team behind the goal line, the ball is placed on its 1-yard line. See 7-4-5 and Note.

Article 3   If an official inadvertently sounds his whistle during a play, the ball becomes dead immediately:

(a) If the ball is in player possession, the team in possession may elect to put the ball in play where it has been declared dead or to replay the down.

(b) If the ball is a loose ball resulting from a fumble, backward pass, or illegal pass, the team last in possession may elect to put the ball in play at the spot possession was lost or to replay the down.

(c) If the ball is a loose ball resulting from a legal forward pass, a free kick, or a scrimmage kick, the ball is returned to the previous spot, and the down is replayed.

(d) If there is a foul by either team during any of the above, penalty enforcement is as usual during a run, forward pass, kick, fumble, and backward pass.

Note: Penalty enforcement following play blown dead by an inadvertent whistle is as ordinary for fouls during runs, passes, kicks, fumbles, and backward passes.

Article 4 When the ball is dead, it is next put in play (7-3-1) at spot designated by official so declaring it. This is usually the spot of the ball when his whistle sounded, but may be some other spot, in case Referee is informed by an official that the ball should have been dead at another spot or in case the rules prescribe otherwise (15-2-3).

Article 5 The ball is not dead because of touching an official who is inbounds or because of a signal by an official other than a whistle.

Note: When a foul occurs, any official observing it immediately sounds his whistle if it is one for which ball remains dead or is dead immediately. Otherwise he signals it by means of dropping his flag (15-1-4-Note) at the spot of the foul unless distance precludes it. In such case, he still indicates the foul in the same manner, but approximates spot, and notes any pertinent circumstances.

Unless a whistle sounds, ball continues in play until otherwise dead (7-4-1).

Section 5   **POSSESSION OF BALL AFTER OUT OF BOUNDS**

Article 1   If any kick, except for a free kick, is out of bounds between the goal lines, ball is next put in play at inbounds spot by the receivers, unless there is a spot of illegal touching nearer kickers' goal line. For free kick out of bounds, see 6-3-1.

Article 2   If it is a play from scrimmage, any possession by offensive team after an out of bounds during fourth down is governed by the location of the necessary line (7-1-3).

Article 3   If a runner (3-27) is out of bounds between goal lines, the ball is next put in play by his team at inbounds spot.

Article 4   If a forward pass is out of bounds between the goal lines, the ball is next put in play by passing team as provided for an incompletion or for an illegal pass. See 8-1-5.

Article 5   If a backward pass is out of bounds between the goal lines, the ball is next in play at the inbounds spot by the team last in possession.

Article 6   A fumble by the offensive team cannot result in an advance by that team if the ball is not recovered in the field of play or end zone.

(a) A fumble that goes forward and out of bounds is to return to that team at the spot of the fumble.

Note: If, on a play from scrimmage, a fumble goes out of bounds forward, the game clock is to be stopped but is to be restarted when the ball can be made ready for play at the spot of the fumble. If the ball goes out of bounds behind the spot of the fumble, game clock is to be stopped and is to be restarted when the ball is snapped for the next down.

 (b) A fumble in the field of play that goes backward and out of bounds belongs to the offense at the out-of-bounds spot.

 (c) A fumble in the field of play that goes forward into the opponent's end zone and over the end line or sideline results in the ball being given over to the defensive team and a touchback awarded.

 (d) A fumble which occurs in a team's own end zone and goes forward into the field of play and out of bounds will result in a safety *if that team provided the impetus that put the ball into the end zone. If the impetus was provided by the opponent, the play will result in a touchback.*

 (e) A fumble which occurs in a team's own end zone or in the field of play and the ball goes out of bounds in the end zone will result in a safety *if that team provided the impetus that put the ball into the end zone. If the impetus was provided by the opponent, the play will result in a touchback.*

Article 7 If a pass, kick, or fumble is out of bounds behind a goal line, Rule 11 governs.

Forward Pass, Backward Pass, Fumble

Rule 8

Forward Pass, Backward Pass, Fumble

Section 1   FORWARD PASS

Article 1   The offensive team may make one forward pass from behind the line during each play from scrimmage provided the ball does not cross the line and return behind line prior to the pass.

(a) Any other forward pass by either team is illegal and is a foul by the passing team.

(b) When any illegal pass is caught or intercepted, the ball may be advanced and the penalty declined.

Penalties:

a) **For a forward pass not from scrimmage: Loss of five yards from the spot of the pass. It is a safety when the spot of the pass is behind the passer's goal line.**

b) **For a second forward pass from behind line, or for a pass that was thrown after the ball returned behind the line: Loss of five yards from the previous spot. Note: See 8-3-1 for intentional grounding.**

c) **For a forward pass from beyond the line: Loss of down and five yards from the spot of the pass (combination penalty). See 14-8-2. See S.N. 3 below.**

■ Supplemental Notes

(1) Eligibility, pass interference, and intentional grounding rules apply to a second pass from behind the line or a forward pass that was thrown from behind the line after the ball returned behind the line. On all other illegal passes, eligibility rules do not apply.

(2) Roughing the passer rules apply on all passes (legal or illegal) from behind the line of scrimmage (12-2-12).

(3) The penalty for a forward pass beyond the line is to be enforced from the spot where the ball is released when the passer's entire body and the ball are beyond the line of scrimmage. This includes either when the passer is airborne or touching the ground.

(4) When a distance penalty in Penalty 8-1-c leaves the ball in advance of the necessary line, it is first-and-10 for the offensive team.

(5) An intentional fumble forward is a forward pass. See 8-4-2-Exc. 1.

(6) For when any legal or illegal pass becomes incomplete, see 8-1-5.

(7) For team possession during a forward pass (loose ball) or when it ends, see 3-2-3.

Article 2 A forward pass from behind the line may be touched or caught by any eligible player. (Pass in flight may be tipped, batted, or deflected in any direction by any eligible player at any time. See 12-1-8).

(a) Defensive players are eligible at all times.

(b) Offensive players who are on either end of the line (other than a center, guard, or tackle) are eligible. See 5-1-4 and 7-2-4.

(c) Offensive players who are at least (legally) one yard behind the line at the snap are eligible, except T-formation quarterbacks. See 7-2-5.

Article 3 An eligible receiver becomes ineligible if he goes out of bounds (prior to or during a pass) and remains ineligible until an eligible receiver or any defensive player touches the pass.

Exception: If the eligible receiver is forced out of bounds because of a foul by a defender, including illegal contact, defensive holding, or defensive pass interference, he will become eligible to legally touch the pass (without prior touching by another eligible receiver or defender) as soon as he legally returns inbounds.

Note: All offensive players become eligible once a pass is touched by an eligible receiver or any defensive players.

Article 4 An ineligible offensive player is one who:

(a) was originally ineligible;

(b) loses his eligibility by going out of bounds;

(c) fails to notify the Referee of being eligible when indicated (7-2-4-Pen. b); or

(d) is a T-formation quarterback who takes his stance behind center,

  (1) receives a hand-to-hand pass or snap from him while moving backward;

  (2) does not receive a hand-to-hand pass or snap from him and is not legally one yard behind the line of scrimmage; or

  (3) ever receives a forward pass (handed or thrown) during a play from scrimmage.

Note: To become an eligible pass receiver, a T-formation quarterback must assume the position of a backfield player (as in a Shotgun, Single Wing, Double Wing, Box or Spread Formation) at least one yard behind his line at the snap. In case of doubt, the penalty for an ineligible player receiving a forward pass shall be enforced.

Article 5 Any forward pass (legal or illegal) becomes incomplete and the ball is dead immediately if the pass strikes the ground or goes out of bounds.

Note: If there is any question by the covering official(s) if a pass is complete, intercepted, or incomplete, it is to be ruled incomplete.

Article 6 A legal forward pass thrown from behind the line is complete and may be advanced if it is:

(a) caught by any offensive player;

(b) caught by any offensive player after it is first touched by any offensive player; or

(c) intercepted by the defense.

Note: If there is any question by the covering official(s) if a pass is complete, intercepted, or incomplete, it is to be ruled incomplete.

Article 7   It is a foul for illegal touching, if a forward pass (legal or illegal):

(a) first touches or is caught by an ineligible offensive player behind, on, or beyond the forward pass line of scrimmage, or

(b) first touches or is caught by an eligible receiver who had gone out of bounds on his own or had been legally forced out of bounds.

Penalty: Loss of five yards from previous spot.

Note 1: If a forward pass (legal or illegal) is caught by an ineligible offensive player, the ball remains alive.

Note 2: If a forward pass (legal or illegal) is caught by an eligible receiver who had gone out of bounds on his own or had been legally forced out of bounds, the ball remains in play.

Note 3: See 8-3-1 for intentional grounding.

Note 4: If a forward pass (legal or illegal) is illegally touched and then is intercepted by B, the interception is legal. 8-1-2-a.

Note 5: If there is illegal touching of a forward pass and also a personal foul for unsportsmanlike conduct by the defensive team, 5 vs. 15 may apply.

■ Supplemental Notes

(1) A ball handed forward (no daylight) to an eligible receiver behind the line is treated as a fumble if he

muffs it (3-21-2-Exc.). A ball handed forward (no daylight) to an ineligible receiver behind the line is treated as a forward pass and remains in play when caught (unless intercepted by B in which case the play continues). See 8-1-5 Note.

(2) The bat of a pass in flight by any player does not end a pass nor does it change the impetus if the act sends it in touch.

(3) If a pass is caught simultaneously by two eligible opposing players who both retain it, the ball belongs to the passers. It is not a simultaneous catch if a player gains control first and retains control, regardless of subsequent joint control with an opponent. If the ball is muffed after simultaneous touching by two such players, all the players of the passing team become eligible to catch the loose ball.

(4) A pass is completed or intercepted if the player has both feet or any other part of his body, except his hands, inbounds prior to and after the catch.

(5) A pass is completed or intercepted, or a loose ball recovered, if the player inbounds would have landed inbounds with both feet but is carried or pushed out of bounds while in possession of the ball in the air or before the second foot touches the ground inbounds by an opponent. The player must maintain possession of the ball when he lands out of bounds.

(6) A pass is not intercepted if the defensive player does not have both feet inbounds prior to the interception (as well as after the interception).

Note: See 11-4-1-Exc., for momentum.

| Section 2 | **PASS INTERFERENCE/INELIGIBLE PLAYER DOWNFIELD** |

| Article 1 | Pass interference can only occur when there is a forward pass thrown from behind the line of scrimmage. This applies regardless of whether the pass crosses the line. |

(a) The restriction for the offensive team begins with the snap.

(b) The restriction for the defensive team begins when the ball leaves the passer's hands.

Article 2   It is a foul when an ineligible offensive player (including a T-formation quarterback), prior to a legal forward pass:

(a) advances beyond his line, after losing contact with an opponent at the line of scrimmage;

(b) loses contact with an opponent downfield after the initial charge and then continues to advance or move laterally; or

(c) moves downfield without contacting an opponent at the line of scrimmage.

The above restrictions end when the ball leaves the passer's hand.

Note: The guideline for officials to use for an ineligible player(s) to be illegally downfield: the offending player must be more than one yard beyond the line of scrimmage prior to the pass.

Penalty: Ineligible offensive player downfield: loss of five yards from previous spot.

Article 3   It is *not* a foul for an ineligible receiver downfield when ineligible receivers:

(a) block an opponent at the line of scrimmage, which drives him downfield, loses the block and remains stationary;

(b) are forced behind their line;

(c) move laterally behind their line (before or after contact of their initial charge) provided they do not advance beyond their line until the ball leaves the passer's hands; or

(d) have legally crossed their line in blocking an opponent (eligible offensive player A1 may complete a pass between them and the offensive line).

Article 4   *After* the ball leaves the passer's hand, ineligible forward-pass receivers can advance:

(a) from behind their line;

(b) from their own line; or

(c) from their initial charge position, provided they do *not* block or contact a defensive player(s) *until* the ball is touched by a player of either team. *Such prior blocking and/or contact is forward-pass interference.*

When an ineligible lineman, who has legally crossed his line in blocking an opponent or a T-formation quarterback is touched by a forward pass while beyond his line, enforcement is for Penalty under 8-1-7.

Article 5   It is pass interference by either team when any player's movement beyond the line of scrimmage significantly hinders the progress of an eligible player or such player's opportunity to catch the ball. Offensive pass-interference rules apply from the time the ball is snapped until the ball is touched. Defensive pass-interference rules apply from the time the ball is thrown until the ball is touched.

Actions that constitute defensive pass interference include but are not limited to:

(a) Contact by a defender who is not playing the ball, and such contact restricts the receiver's opportunity to make the catch.

(b) Playing through the back of a receiver in an attempt to make a play on the ball.

(c) Grabbing a receiver's arm(s) in such a manner that restricts his opportunity to catch a pass.

(d) Extending an arm across the body of a receiver thus restricting his ability to catch a pass, regardless of whether the defender is playing the ball.

(e) Cutting off the path of a receiver by making contact with him without playing the ball.

(f) Hooking a receiver in an attempt to get to the ball in such a manner that it causes the receiver's body to turn prior to the ball arriving.

Actions that do not constitute pass interference include but are not limited to:

(a) Incidental contact by a defender's hands, arms, or body when both players are competing for the ball, or neither player is looking for the ball. If there is any question whether contact is incidental, the ruling shall be no interference.
(b) Inadvertent tangling of feet when both players are playing the ball or neither player is playing the ball.
(c) Contact that would normally be considered pass interference, but the pass is clearly uncatchable by the involved players.
(d) Laying a hand on a receiver that does not restrict the receiver in an attempt to make a play on the ball.
(e) Contact by a defender who has gained position on a receiver in an attempt to catch the ball.

Actions that constitute offensive pass interference include but are not limited to:

(a) Blocking downfield by an offensive player prior to the ball being touched.
(b) Initiating contact with a defender by shoving or pushing off, thus creating a separation, in an attempt to catch a pass.
(c) Driving through a defender who has established a position on the field.

Actions that do not constitute offensive pass interference include but are not limited to:

(a) Incidental contact by a receiver's hands, arms, or body when both players are competing for the ball or neither player is looking for the ball.

(b) Inadvertent touching of feet when both players are playing the ball or neither player is playing the ball.

(c) Contact that would normally be considered pass interference, but the ball is clearly uncatchable by involved players.

Note 1: If there is any question whether player contact is incidental, the ruling should be no interference.

Note 2: Defensive players have as much right to the path of the ball as eligible offensive players.

Note 3: Pass interference for both teams ends when the pass is touched.

Note 4: There can be no pass interference at or behind the line of scrimmage, but defensive actions such as tackling a receiver can still result in a five-yard penalty for defensive holding, if accepted.

Note 5: Whenever a team presents an apparent punting formation, defensive pass interference is not to be called for action on the end man on the line of scrimmage, or an eligible receiver behind the line of scrimmage who is aligned or in motion more than one yard outside the end man on the line. Defensive holding, such as tackling a receiver, still can be called and result in a five-yard penalty from the previous spot, if accepted. Offensive pass interference rules still apply.

Penalties:

(a) **Pass interference by offense: Loss of 10 yards from previous spot.**

(b) **Pass interference by defense: First down for offensive team at the spot of any such foul. If the interference is also a personal foul (12-2), the usual distance penalty for such a foul (whether the pass is complete or incomplete) is also enforced (from spot to foul). If the interference is behind the defensive goal line, it is first down for the offensive team on**

the defense's 1-yard line, or, if the previous spot
was inside the 2-yard line, then halfway between
the previous spot and the goal line.

See 8-3-3 and 4 for optional penalty in case of a personal
foul (12-2) by opponents prior to any completion or
interception.

Section 3 **FOULS ON PASSES AND ENFORCEMENT**

Article 1 Intentional grounding will be called when a passer,
facing an imminent loss of yardage because of pressure
from the defense, throws a forward pass without a realistic chance of completion.

*Note 1: Intentional grounding will not be called when a
passer, while outside the tackle position and facing an
imminent loss of yardage, throws a forward pass that lands
near or beyond the line of scrimmage, even if no offensive
player(s) have a realistic chance to catch the ball (including
if the ball lands out of bounds over the sideline or endline).*

*Note 2: A passer, after delaying his passing action for strate-
gic purposes, is prohibited from throwing the ball to the
ground in front of him, even though he is under no pressure
from defensive rusher(s).*

*Note 3: A player under center is permitted to stop the game
clock legally to save time if immediately upon receiving the
snap he begins a continuous throwing motion and throws
the ball directly forward into the ground.*

*Note 4: Intentional grounding should not be called if the
passer initiates his passing motion toward an eligible
receiver and then is significantly affected by physical
contact from a defensive player causing the pass to fall
incomplete.*

*Note 5: When the ball, either in possession or loose, leaves
the area bordered by the tackles, this area no longer exists.*

All intentional grounding rules apply as if the passer is outside this area (as stated in Note 1 above).

Note 6: A realistic chance of completion is defined as a pass that is thrown in the direction and the vicinity of an eligible receiver.

Penalty: For intentional grounding: loss of down and 10 yards from the previous spot, or if foul occurs more than 10 yards from line of scrimmage or where it is more advantageous to the defense, loss of down at spot of foul, or safety if passer is in his end zone when ball is thrown.

Article 2   If there is a foul by either team from the time of the snap until a forward pass from behind the line ends, the penalty is enforced from the previous spot.

Note: A forward pass in flight that is controlled or caught may only be thrown backwards. If thrown forward it is considered illegally batting a loose ball and the penalty is enforced from the previous spot.

Exceptions:

1) Pass interference by the defense is enforced from the spot of the foul.
2) A personal foul prior to interception or completion of a pass from behind the line, enforcement is from the spot chosen (8-3-3, 4).
3) It is a safety when the offensive team commits a foul behind its own goal line.

Article 3   When the defense commits a personal foul (or unsportsmanlike foul) **prior** to a completion of a legal forward pass from behind the line, the offense shall have the choice to take:

(a) the usual penalty—15 yards from the previous spot; or
(b) a 15-yard penalty enforced from the spot where the ball is dead.

Exception: If the passing team is fouled and loses possession after a completion, enforcement is from the previous spot and the ball will be retained by the offended team after enforcement of the personal foul.

Article 4   When the offense commits a personal foul (or unsportsmanlike foul) prior to an interception of a forward pass or the recovery of a backward pass or fumble, the defense will have a 15-yard penalty enforced from the spot where the ball is dead.

Exception: If the intercepting or recovering team is fouled and loses possession after the interception or recovery, enforcement is from the spot where the interception or recovery occurred, and the ball will be retained by the offended team after the enforcement of the personal foul.

Note 1: When the dead ball spot is normally a touchback, enforce from the goal line.

Note 2: Personal fouls do not include holding, illegal use of hands, illegal batting, kicking the ball, or tripping. See Rule 12-2.

Article 5   If there is a foul by the defense from the start of the snap until a legal forward pass ends, it is *not* offset by an incompletion by the offensive team.

Exception: Any foul by the offensive team would offset a foul by the defensive team (14-3-1).

Section 4   **BACKWARD PASS AND FUMBLE**

Article 1   A runner may pass backward at any time (3-21-4).

(a) An offensive player may catch a backward pass or recover it after the pass touches the ground and advance.

(b) A defensive player may catch a backward pass or recover it after the pass touches the ground and advance.

Note: A direct snap from center is treated as a backward pass. A muffed hand-to-hand snap from center is treated as a fumble by the quarterback.

Exception: See actions to conserve time (4-3-10).

Article 2 Any player of either team may recover or catch and advance a fumble:

(a) before the fumble strikes the ground; or
(b) after the fumble strikes the ground.

Note: A fumble is legally recovered or caught in bounds by a player if the player had both feet in bounds prior to the recovery or catch. See 7-5-6 for fumble out of bounds and 11-4-1-Exc. for a fumble in end zone following intercepting momentum.

Exceptions:

1) If a runner *intentionally* fumbles forward, it is a forward pass (3-21-2-a and Note 4).

2) If a fourth-down fumble occurs during a play from scrimmage and the fumbling player recovers the ball, he only:

   a) may advance; or
   b) hand and/or pass the ball forward or backward (as prescribed by rule).

3) If a fourth-down fumble occurs during a play from scrimmage and the recovery or catch is by another offensive player, the spot of the next snap is:

   a) the spot of the fumble, unless
   b) the spot of recovery is behind the spot of the fumble and it is then at the spot of recovery. See 8-4-3.

4) If a fourth-down fumble occurs during a play from scrimmage and the ball rolls out of bounds from field of play, the ball is next put in play at the spot of the fumble, unless the spot out of bounds is behind the spot of the fumble, then it is at that spot (Rule 7-5-6).

■ Supplemental Note

After the two-minute warning, when any fumble occurs during a down (including Try), the fumbled ball may only be advanced by the offensive player who fumbled the ball, or any member of the defensive team. See 11-3-1-b.

Note: When a backward pass or fumble is a simultaneous or hidden ball recovery by two opposing players, the ball is awarded to the team making the pass or fumble.

Article 3   If a backward pass goes out of bounds between the goal lines, the ball is next put in play at the inbounds spot by the team in last possession. The ball is dead (7-5-5). Rule 11 governs if a backward pass is declared dead behind the goal line.

Article 4   When a foul occurs during a backward pass or fumble, the basic spot of enforcement is the spot of the fumble or the spot of the backward pass. If the offensive team fouls behind the spot of the fumble or backward pass, the spot of enforcement is the spot of the foul (14-1-5).

Exception: When the spot of the backward pass or fumble is behind the line (including A's end zone) and either team fouls during the loose ball, the spot of enforcement is the previous spot, even if B's foul is in A's end zone. See 11-4-2 for safety (offensive foul in own end zone).

Note: When the spot of the fumble or backward pass is beyond the line, a defensive foul during the backward pass or fumble occurring anywhere is enforced from the spot of the fumble or backward pass.

■ Supplemental Notes

(1) When a backward pass or fumble touches a goal post, ball is dead as it is out of bounds.

(2) For team possession during a backward pass or fumble (loose ball) or when it ends, see 3-2-3 and 3-21-4.

(3) After a backward pass or fumble touches the ground, any player may legally block or otherwise use his hands or arms to push or pull an opponent out of the way, but only in an actual personal attempt to recover (12-1-2, 3).

(4) A backward pass going out of bounds during the last two minutes of a half stops the game clock (4-3-10-S.N. 6).

(5) For fumbles forward out of bounds or unrecovered in the field of play or in the end zone, see 7-5-6.

Scrimmage Kick

Rule 9

Scrimmage Kick

Section 1 **KICK FROM SCRIMMAGE**

Article 1 The kicking team, behind the scrimmage line, may:

(a) punt;
(b) dropkick; or
(c) placekick.

Penalty: For a punt, dropkick, or placekick not kicked from behind the line of scrimmage: 10 yards from the spot of the kick.

Note: This is not considered illegally kicking the ball.

Article 2 If the receivers recover any kick, they may advance. For fair catch exception, see 10-1-2.

Note: For team possession during a scrimmage kick (loose ball) or when it ends, see 3-2-3.

Article 3 During a kick from scrimmage only the end men, as eligible receivers on the line of scrimmage at the time of the snap, are permitted to go beyond the line before the ball is kicked.

Exception: An eligible receiver who, at the snap, is aligned or in motion behind the line and more than one yard outside the end man on his side of the line, clearly making him the outside receiver, replaces that end man as the player eligible to go downfield after the snap. All other members of the kicking team must remain at the line of scrimmage until the ball has been kicked.

Penalty: Loss of five yards from the previous spot for leaving before the ball is kicked.

Note: The guideline for officials to use for an ineligible player(s) to be illegally downfield: he must be more than one yard beyond the line of scrimmage, prior to the kick from scrimmage.

Article 4   No player of the kickers may illegally touch a scrimmage kick before it has been touched by a receiver (first touching).

Exception: When a kick is from behind the line, any touching on or behind the line by any offensive player is legal and any player may recover and advance (See 3-27-2-S.N. 2).

Penalty: For illegal touching of a scrimmage kick: Receivers' ball at any spot of illegal touching or possession. Officials' time out when the ball is declared dead. This illegal touch does not offset a foul by the receivers during the down. See 4-3-1; 4-3-7; and 14-3-1-Exc. 4.

Note: When any player of the kicking team (inside the receiver's 5-yard line) illegally recovers or catches a punt or failed field goal attempt kicked from inside the receiver's 20-yard line (See 11-5-1, 2, 3), carries the ball directly across the receiver's goal line or his body contacts the end zone, it is a touchback. There is no penalty for delay. (This creates Exception to 4-3-9-j) and the ball is not dead (7-4-1-j).

Article 5   No player of the kicker's team, who has been out of bounds, may touch or recover a scrimmage kick beyond the line until it has been touched by a kicking-team player who has not been out of bounds or until after it has been touched by the receiving team.

Penalty: Loss of five yards from the previous spot. If the illegal touching is inside the receiver's 5-yard line, the receiving team may elect to take a touchback.

Article 6   A ball is dead if the kickers recover a kick made from behind the line (other than one recovered on or behind the line unless a Try-kick) (9-1-4-Exc.).

Note: When the kickers recover a legal kick from scrimmage after it has first been touched by the receiving team beyond the line, it is first-and-10 for A or if it is recovered by the kickers in the receiver's end zone, it is a touchdown for the kickers. See 7-1-1-c-d and 9-1-4-Exc.

Article 7   If a kick from behind the line is touched in the immediate vicinity of the neutral zone or behind A's line by B, such touching does not make A eligible to recover the kick beyond the line.

Article 8   Any touching behind the line by a kicking-team player is legal, even if the kick crosses the line and returns behind the line before touching a receiver beyond the line.

Article 9   When a legal kick is simultaneously recovered anywhere by two eligible opposing players, or if it is lying on the field of play with no player attempting to recover, it is awarded to the receivers. See 7-4-2.

Article 10   Ordinarily there is no distinction between a player touching a ball or being touched by it.

Exception: If he is pushed or blocked into a kick by an opponent, he is NOT considered to have touched the ball (3-14-3-Notes).

Note: In order for a player to be considered as not touching the ball, he must be blocked from a passive position into the ball. If he is engaged and is blocking his opponent and he contacts the ball, he is deemed to have touched it.

Article 11   During a kick a kicking team player, after he has crossed his scrimmage line, may use his hands to ward off, push, or pull aside a receiver who is legally or illegally attempting to obstruct him. See 12-1-2-Exc. 3, and Note.

Note: See 12-2-13 for prohibited low blocks during kicks.

Article 12   When a scrimmage kick from behind the line is recovered by the kicking team behind the line, the kicking team may advance (see 3-27-2, S.N. 2).

Exception: If the kicking team recovers a kick behind the line during a Try-kick the ball is dead immediately (11-3-1).

Article 13   If a scrimmage kick that has not been touched by a player of the receiving team crosses the receiver's goal line from the impetus of the kick, the ball is dead immediately when it touches the ground or a player of the kicking team on or behind the receiver's goal line. If the scrimmage kick is a failed field-goal attempt from inside the receiver's 20-yard line or a punt, it is a touchback. If the scrimmage kick is a failed field-goal attempt from the receiver's 20-yard line or beyond the receiver's 20-yard line, the receiving team takes possession of the ball at the spot of the kick.

(a) On a punt there is a spot of illegal touching by the kickers outside the receivers' 20-yard line; receiver's ball at spot of illegal touch.

(b) The receivers, after gaining possession, advance with the ball into the field of play; receiver's ball at dead-ball spot.

(c) Kickers recover in end zone after receivers first touch ball in field of play; touchdown for kickers.

(d) Kickers recover in end zone after receivers first touch ball in end zone; touchdown for kickers.

(e) On a punt, the ball goes out of bounds in the field of play after being touched by a receiver in the end zone or field of play; receiving team's ball at inbounds spot.

(f) On a missed field-goal attempt, the ball goes out of bounds in the field of play after being touched by a receiver in the end zone; touchback.

> *Note: Receiving team players may advance any kick (scrimmage or unsuccessful field goal attempt) whether the ball crosses the receiver's goal line. Rule 9, Section 1 (Kicks From Scrimmage) applies until the receiving team has gained possession. See 11-5-2.*

Article 14   If a punt or missed field-goal attempt from inside the receiver's 20-yard line touches the receiver's goal posts or crossbar either before or after touching a player of either team, it is a touchback. See 3-20-2 and 11-5-1.

Article 15   If a scrimmage kick *touches the kicker's goal post or crossbar* (irrespective of where it was made from, or how it occurred), it is a safety. Goal post is out of bounds. See 11-4-1-b.

Article 16   For a scrimmage kick out of bounds between goal lines, see 7-5-1. If the kick becomes dead behind a goal line, Rule 11-6 governs.

Article 17   If there is a foul from the time of the snap until a legal scrimmage-kick ends, enforcement is from the previous spot. This includes a foul during a run prior to the legal kick (14-1-13-S.N. 1), and running into or roughing the kicker (12-2-6). If the offensive team commits a foul in its own end zone, it is a safety.

Exception 1: If a foul by the kicking team occurs during a scrimmage kick play prior to a player of the receiving team securing possession of the ball, the offended team will have the option of taking the penalty at the previous spot and replaying the down or adding the penalty yardage on to the end of the play.

Exception 2: Illegal touching of kick, fair catch interference, interference with opportunity, invalid fair catch signal, or personal foul (blocking) after fair catch signal are all enforced from the spot of the foul.

Exception 3: If the receiving team commits a foul after the ball is kicked (ball crosses the scrimmage line) during a scrimmage down and the receivers possess and thereafter keep the kicked ball, throughout the remainder of the down, the penalty for their infraction will be ruled as a foul after possession (post-possession) and must be assessed from:

1) The spot where possession was gained;
2) The spot where ball becomes dead; or
3) The spot of the foul.

Note: If there is a spot of illegal touch, it is not used.

Exception 4: In cases of illegal touch by kicker, and a foul by the receiving team during the kick, if the receiving team then loses possession, the ball reverts to the receivers and the penalty must be assessed from:

1) The spot where possession was gained;
2) The spot of the foul.

Note: The spot of illegal touch is not used.

Article 18   During a punt (prior to a change of possession), if a kicking-team player goes out of bounds voluntarily (without being contacted) it is a foul.

Penalty: Loss of five yards from the previous spot.

Fair
Catch

Rule 10

Fair Catch

Section 1   **FAIR CATCH**

Article 1   A fair-catch signal is valid if it is made while the kick is in flight by a player who is beyond the line of scrimmage, who fully extends one arm above his helmet and waves it from side to side. A receiver is permitted to legally raise his hand(s) to his helmet to shield his eyes from the sun, but is not permitted to raise them above his helmet except to signal for a fair catch. If a player raises his hands above his shoulder(s) for any other reason, it is an invalid fair-catch signal.

Penalty: For invalid fair-catch signal: Snap by receivers five yards behind the spot of the signal.

Article 2   If a receiver signals (valid or invalid) for a fair catch during any kick except one which does not cross the line, the ball is dead when caught by any receiver (Article 2, Exception). If the catcher did not signal, the ball is put in play by the receivers at the spot of the catch. See 10-1-6.

Exception: Any receiver may recover and advance after a fair-catch signal if the kick:

1) touches one of the kickers.

Note: Undue advance by any receiver who catches (except as provided in above Exception) is delay of the game but does not preclude the fair catch. No specific distance is specified for undue advance as the ball is dead at the spot of the catch (3-9-1) when caught (time out). If the catcher comes to a reasonable stop, there is no penalty for delay. Any penalty is enforced from the spot of the catch.

Article 3   If a player signals (valid or invalid) for a fair catch, until the ball touches another player he may not:

(a) block; or
(b) initiate contact with one of the kickers.

Penalty: For illegal block after a fair-catch signal. Snap by receivers 15 yards from the spot of the foul. (Personal Foul.)

Article 4   During any kick (except one which fails to cross the scrimmage line), if any receiver could reach the kick in flight, no player of the kickers shall interfere with either:

(a) the receiver;
(b) the ball; or
(c) the receiver's path to the ball.

Penalty (a): For fair-catch interference following a signal: Loss of 15 yards from the spot of the foul. Fair catch also awarded irrespective of a catch. See Article 5-Note, and Article 6. (Personal Foul.)

Penalty (b): For interference with the opportunity to make a catch (no prior signal made): Loss of 15 yards from the spot of the foul and offended team is entitled to put the ball in play by a snap from scrimmage. See 4-3-11-h. (Personal foul if there is contact.)

■ Supplemental Notes

(1) A receiver running toward a kick in flight has the right of way and opponents must get out of his path to the ball. Otherwise it is interference irrespective of any contact or catch or whether any signal (valid or invalid) is given or not.

(2) After a valid fair-catch signal, the opportunity to make a catch does not end when a kick is muffed. The player who signaled fair catch must have a

reasonable opportunity to catch the ball before it hits the ground without being interfered with by the members of the kicking team.

(3) An intentional muff forward prior to a catch in order to gain ground is an illegal bat (see 12-1-8).

Article 5   After a receiver has made a fair catch following a valid signal, an opponent:

(a) may not tackle him;

(b) may not block him; and

(c) must avoid contact with him.

Penalty: For illegal contact with the maker of a fair catch: Loss of 15 yards from the mark of the catch (snap or free kick). See 6-1-3-Note.

Note: A receiver may make or be awarded a fair catch after fair-catch interference in his end zone. However, it is considered a touchback, and no fair-catch kick is awarded. After a receiver has made a fair catch in the end zone and there is then illegal contact with the maker of the fair catch, the 15-yard penalty is enforced from the receiver's 20-yard line, and fair catch is awarded.

Article 6   When a fair catch is declared for a team, the captain must choose (and his first choice is not revocable) either:

(a) A fair-catch kick (drop kick or place kick without a tee) must be made on or behind the mark of the catch (3-9-1 and 11-5-3), or

(b) A snap to put the ball in play.

Note: If the fair catch is made or awarded outside the inbounds lines, the ball is next put in play at the nearest inbounds line.

■ **Supplemental Notes**

    (1) If, with time remaining, receiver signals and makes a fair catch, receiving-team captain has option of attempting a fair-catch kick or putting ball in play by a snap from scrimmage.

    (2) If, with time remaining, receiver does not signal for a fair catch, and he is interfered with, receiving team will be awarded a 15-yard penalty but must put the ball in play by a snap from scrimmage.

    (3) If, with time remaining, receiver signals for a fair catch, and is interfered with, receiving team will be awarded a 15-yard penalty and has option of a fair-catch kick or putting ball in play by a snap from scrimmage.

    (4) If time expired on the play and receiver signals and makes a fair catch, receiving team may elect to extend with a fair-catch kick. There is no option to snap from scrimmage.

    (5) If time expired on the play and receiver does not signal for a fair catch, and he is interfered with, receiving team will be awarded a 15-yard penalty and an option to extend, but must put the ball in play by a snap from scrimmage.

    (6) If time expired on the play and receiver signals for a fair catch, and is interfered with, receiving team will be awarded a 15-yard penalty and has the option to extend with a fair-catch kick or may put the ball in play by a snap from scrimmage for the period to be extended.

Scoring

Rule 11

Scoring

Section 1 VALUE OF SCORES

Article 1   The team that scores the greater number of points during the entire game is the winner. Points are scored as follows:

(a) Touchdown . . . . 6 points
(b) Field Goal . . . . 3 points
(c) Safety . . . . 2 points
(d) Successful try after touchdown . . . . . 1 or 2 points

Note: If a team forfeits a game, the opponent will be declared the winner by a score of 2-0, but the points will not be added to the winning team's record for purposes of offensive production on tie-breakers

Article 2   If the score is tied at the end of four periods, the game will be extended by an overtime period (see Rule 16).

Section 2 TOUCHDOWN

Article 1   It is a touchdown (3-38):

(a) when a runner advances from the field of play and the ball touches the opponents' goal line (plane); or
(b) while inbounds any player catches or recovers a loose ball (3-2-3) on or behind the opponents' goal line.

■ Supplemental Notes

(1) The ball is automatically dead at the instant of legal player possession on, above, or behind the opponents' goal line.
(2) The Referee may award a touchdown when a palpably unfair act deprives the offended team of one.

(3) For a foul after a touchdown (between downs), see
3-11-2-a and 14-5.

Section 3   **TRY**

Article 1   After a touchdown, the scoring team is allowed a Try.
This Try is an attempt to score one or two additional
points, during one scrimmage down with the spot of
snap:

(a) anywhere between the inbounds lines and
(b) which is also two or more yards from the defensive
team's goal line.

*Note 1: All general rules for fourth-down fumbles apply to
the Try (See 8-4-2-Exc. 2), and the game clock will not
run.*

*Note 2: If the ball has been declared ready for play by the
Referee, and the offensive team wants to change the location
of the ball, they can do so by calling a time out.*

During this Try:

*Note 3: See 7-2-3 for restriction applicable to Team B for-
mation at snap.*

(a) if a Try-kick is good, one point is scored. (The conditions of 11-5-1 must be met.) If a kick cannot
score, the ball becomes dead as soon as failure is
evident.
(b) if a Try results in what would ordinarily be a touchdown by the offense, two points are awarded. If a
touchdown is not scored, the Try is over at the end
of the play or if there is a change of possession.
(c) if there is no kick and the Try results in what would
ordinarily be a safety by the defense, one point is
awarded to the offensive team.

Article 2   The Try begins when the Referee sounds his whistle for
play to start.

Note: See 3-11-1-d-Exc. for a foul after a touchdown and before the whistle.

Article 3   During a Try:

(a) if any play or a foul by the offense would ordinarily result in a touchback or loss of down, the Try is unsuccessful and there shall be no replay.

(b) if any play or a foul by the defense would ordinarily result in a safety, one point is awarded the offensive team.

(c) if a foul by the defense does not permit the Try to be attempted, the down is replayed and the offended team has the option to have the distance penalty assessed on the next Try or on the ensuing kickoff.

(d) if the defensive team commits a foul and the Try is attempted and is unsuccessful, the offensive team may either accept the penalty yardage to be assessed or decline the distance penalty before the down is replayed.

(e) all fouls committed by the defense on a successful Try will result in the distance penalty being assessed on the ensuing kickoff or retry B1.

(f) if there is a false start, encroachment, or a neutral zone infraction which normally causes play to be whistled dead during ordinary scrimmage plays, they are to be handled the same way during Try situations. Blow whistle immediately. (See 7-2-2 and 7-3-4).

Note: See 12-3-1-a, k, l, m, p, that apply during a Try.

Article 4   If fouls are signalled against both teams during a Try, it must be replayed (14-3-1).

Article 5   During a Try the defensive team can never score. When it gains possession, the ball is dead immediately.

Article 6   After a Try the team on defense during the Try shall receive (6-1-1-b).

Section 4   SAFETY

Article 1   When an impetus by a team sends the ball in touch behind its own goal, it is a safety if the ball is either:

(a) dead in the end zone in its possession; or
(b) out of bounds behind the goal line.

Exception: If a defensive player, in the field of play, intercepts a pass or catches or recovers a fumble, backward pass, scrimmage kick, free kick or fair catch kick, and his original momentum carries him into his end zone where the ball is declared dead in his team's possession, the ball belongs to the defensive team at the spot where the ball was intercepted, caught, or recovered.

(a) If a player of the team which intercepts, catches, or recovers the ball commits a foul in the end zone, it may be a safety.
(b) If a player who intercepts, catches, or recovers the ball throws a completed illegal forward pass from the end zone, the ball remains alive. If his opponent intercepts the illegal pass thrown from the end zone, the ball remains alive. If he scores, it is a touchdown.
(c) If a player of the team which intercepts, catches, or recovers the ball commits a foul in the field of play and the ball becomes dead in the end zone, the basic spot is the spot of the change of possession with momentum.
(d) If spot where possession changed is inside B's one-yard line, ball is to be spotted at B1.

■ Supplemental Notes

(1) The impetus is always attributed to the offense…unless the defense creates a new momentum, by a muff of a ball which is at rest or nearly at rest, illegal batting of a ball, or illegally kicking a ball that sends it in touch. (3-14-3).

(2) See 8-1-1-S.N. 2 for Exceptions to (b) of 11-4-1, when there is an incompletion or pass violation by the offense behind its goal line during a forward pass from behind the line.

Article 2   It is a safety when the offense commits a foul (anywhere) and the spot of enforcement is behind its own goal line.

Article 3   After a safety, the team scored upon must next put the ball in play by a free kick (punt, dropkick or placekick). No tee can be used. See 6-1-2, 3.

Exception: Extension of period (4-3-11-i).

Section 5   **FIELD GOAL**

Article 1   A field goal is scored when all of the following conditions are met:

(a) The kick must be a placekick or dropkick made by the offense from behind the line of scrimmage or from the spot of a fair catch (fair-catch kick).

(b) The ball must not touch the ground or any player of the offensive team before it passes through the goal.

(c) The entire ball must pass through the goal. In case wind or other forces cause it to return through the goal, it must have struck the ground or some object or person before returning.

Note 1: See 7-2-3 for restriction applicable to Team B formation at snap.

Article 2   All field goals attempted and missed when the spot of the kick is beyond the 20-yard line will result in the defensive team taking possession of the ball at the spot of the kick. On any field goal attempted and missed when the spot of the kick is on or inside the 20-yard line, the ball will revert to the defensive team at the 20-yard line.

Exception 1: If a field-goal attempt is missed and the ball is touched or possessed by the receivers beyond the line of scrimmage in the field of play, the ball will not come back to the spot of kick. All general rules for a kick from scrimmage will apply. If a foul occurs during the missed field-goal attempt, Rule 9-1-17 governs.

Exception 2: If a blocked field goal attempted from anywhere on the field is recovered behind the line of scrimmage by a defensive player and is not advanced, or if the blocked field-goal attempt goes out of bounds behind the line of scrimmage, it is the receiving team's ball at that spot.

■ Supplemental Notes

(1) If a missed field goal is first touched by the receivers beyond the line in the field of play and the ball then goes out of bounds, it is the receivers' ball at the out-of-bounds spot.

(2) If a missed field goal does not touch a receiver in the end zone and the ball then bounces back into the field of play, it is the receivers' ball at the spot of the kick if they did not touch the ball in the field of play (touchback if kick is made from inside B20).

(3) If on a missed field goal the ball first touches a receiver in the end zone and returns to the field of play where it is not covered and then declared dead,

the ball belongs to B at the spot of the kick (touchback if kick is made from inside B20).

(4) If the receivers first touch a missed field goal anywhere beyond the line of scrimmage and the kickers recover, the ball belongs to the kickers at the spot of the recovery. If in the end zone, it is a touchdown.

Exception: If a receiver is the first to touch a missed field goal in the field of play, and the ball then rolls into the end zone where it is declared dead (no new impetus) in possession of B, it is a touchback.

Note: See 12-3-1-a, k, l, m that apply during a field-goal attempt.

Article 3   On a field-goal attempt (10-1-6) following a fair catch, all general rules apply as for a field-goal attempt from scrimmage. The clock starts when the ball is kicked.

■ **Supplemental Note 1**

(a) The fair-catch-kick line for the kicking team is the yard line through the most forward point from which the ball is kicked.
(b) The fair-catch-kick line for the receiving team is the yard line 10 yards in advance of the kicking team's fair-catch-kick line.

■ **Supplemental Note 2**

The game clock starts when the ball is kicked, independent of the time of game.

Exception: The ball is no longer a free-kick ball. The kicking team can't get the ball unless it has been first touched or possessed by the receivers.

Article 4   No artificial media shall be permitted to assist in the execution of a field goal and/or Try-kick attempt after a touchdown.

Article 5   After a field goal, the team scored upon will receive.

Section 6   **TOUCHBACK**

Note: A touchback, while not a score, is included in this rule because, like scoring plays, it is a case of a ball dead in touch (3-14-2).

Article 1   When an impetus (3-14-3) by a team sends a ball in touch behind its opponents' goal line, it is a touchback:

(a) if the ball is dead in the opponents' possession in their end zone;

(b) if the ball is out of bounds behind the goal line (see 7-5-6-c);

(c) if the impetus was a scrimmage kick unless there is a spot of first touching by the kickers outside the receivers' 20-yard line or if the receivers after gaining possession advance with the ball into the field of play (9-1-13-b); or

(d) if any legal kick touches the receivers' goal posts or crossbar other than one which scores a field goal.

Note: The impetus is not from a kick if a muff, bat, juggle, or illegal kick of any kicked ball (by a player of either team) creates a new momentum which sends it in touch. See 3-14-1-Note, for a specific ball-in-touch ruling.

Article 2   It is a touchback:

(a) when the kickers interfere with a fair catch behind the receivers' goal line (10-1-5-Note and 10-1-2); or

(b) when the kickers first touch a punt kicked from anywhere in the field of play, or missed field-goal attempt from inside the receiver's 20-yard line, behind the receiver's goal line (9-1-13 and 11-5-1, 2, 3).

(c) when a kicking-team player inside the receiver's 5-yard line illegally recovers or catches a punt or missed field-goal attempt from inside the receiver's 20-yard line (9-1-13 and 11-5-1, 2, 3), and carries the ball directly across the receiver's goal line (9-1-4-Note); or his body touches the end zone (See 9-1-4-Note).

Article 3 When the spot of enforcement for a foul by the defense is behind the offensive goal line, the distance penalty is enforced from the goal line (14-1-11). See 8-4-4 for exception.

Article 4 After a touchback, the touchback team next snaps from its 20 (any point between the inbounds lines and the forward point of the ball on that line).

Player Conduct

Rule 12

Player Conduct

Section 1   **BLOCKING, USE OF HANDS, ARMS, AND BODY**

Article 1

A player of either team may block (obstruct or impede) an opponent at any time, provided that the act is not:

(a) pass interference
(b) illegal contact
(c) fair-catch interference
(d) clipping against a non-runner
(e) an illegal chop block
(f) an illegal crackback block
(g) an illegal low block during a free kick, scrimmage kick, or after a change of possession
(h) unnecessary roughness
(i) interference with a passer
(j) an illegal cut block
(k) interference with a kicker
(l) offensive or defensive holding
(m) illegal use of hands
(n) tripping

Article 2

An offensive player cannot obstruct or impede an opponent by grasping him with his hands or encircling any part of a defender's body with his arms, except in the following situations:

(a) If he is a runner. A runner may ward off opponents with his hands and arms. He also may lay his hand on a teammate or push him into an opponent, but he may not grasp or hold on to a teammate; or

(b) During a loose ball. An offensive player may use his hands/arms legally to block or otherwise push or pull an opponent out of the way in a **personal** attempt to recover the ball. See specific fumble, pass, or kick

rules and especially 6-2-5-S-N. 1; or

(c) During a kick. A kicking-team player may use his hands/arms to ward off or to push or pull aside a receiver who is legally or illegally attempting to obstruct his attempt to proceed downfield; or

(d) During a legal block.

Penalty: For illegal use of hands, arms, or body by the offense: Loss of 10 yards.

Article 3 An offensive player is permitted to block an opponent by contacting him with his head, shoulders, hands, and/or outer surface of the forearm, or with any other part of his body.

A blocker may use his arms, or open or closed hands, to contact an opponent on or outside the opponent's frame (the body of an opponent below the neck that is presented to the blocker). If a blocker's arms or hands are outside an opponent's frame, it is a foul if the blocker materially restricts him. The blocker immediately must work to bring his hands inside the opponent's frame, and as the play develops, the blocker is permitted to work for and maintain his position against an opponent, provided that he does not illegally clip or illegally push from behind.

Article 4 An offensive blocker cannot:

(a) thrust his hands forward above the frame of an opponent to contact him on the neck, face, or head (Note: Contact in close-line play that is not prolonged and sustained is not a foul);

(b) charge or fall into the back of an opponent above the waist, or use his hands or arms to push an opponent from behind in a manner that affects his movement, except in close-line play (the guideline for officials to use for illegal use of hands in the back above the waist is: if either hand is on the back, it is a foul. If both hands are on the opponent's side, it is not a foul);

Note: The prohibition applies to a player of the kicking team while the ball is in flight during a scrimmage kick.

(c) use his hands or arms to materially restrict an opponent or alter the defender's path or angle of pursuit. Material restrictions include but are not limited to:

    (i) grabbing or tackling an opponent;
    (ii) hooking, jerking, twisting, or turning him; or
    (iii) pulling him to the ground.

Penalty: For holding, illegal use of hands, arms, or body by the offense: Loss of 10 yards.

Blocking notes:

1. When a defensive player is held by an offensive player during the following situations, offensive holding will not be called:

    (a) if the runner is being tackled simultaneously by another defensive player;
    (b) if the runner simultaneously goes out of bounds;
    (c) if a fair catch is made simultaneously;
    (d) if the action clearly occurs after a forward pass has been thrown to a receiver beyond the line of scrimmage;
    (e) if the action occurs away from the point of attack and not within close-line play;
    (f) if a free kick results in a touchback;
    (g) if a scrimmage kick simultaneously becomes a touchback;
    (h) if the action is part of a double-team block in close-line play.

Exception 1: Holding will be called if the opponent is pulled to the ground by one or both of the blockers.

   (i) if, during a defensive charge, a defensive player uses a "rip" technique that puts an offensive player in a position that would normally be holding.

Exception 2: Holding will be called if the defender's feet are taken away from him by the offensive player's action.

2. If a blocker falls on or pushes down a defender whose momentum is carrying him to the ground, offensive holding will not be called unless the blocker prevents the defender from rising from the ground.

3. If the official has not seen the entire action that sends a defender to the ground, offensive holding will not be called.

Article 5 No offensive player may:

   (a) lift a runner to his feet or pull him in any direction at any time; or

   (b) use interlocking interference, by grasping a teammate or by using his hands or arms to encircle the body of a teammate; or

   (c) trip an opponent; or

   (d) push or throw his body against a teammate to aid him in an attempt to obstruct an opponent or to recover a loose ball.

Penalty: For assisting the runner or for interlocking interference: Loss of 10 yards.

Penalty: For tripping, holding, illegal use of hands, arms, or body by the offense: Loss of 10 yards.

Article 6 A defensive player may not tackle or hold any opponent other than a runner. Otherwise, he may use his hands, arms, or body only to defend or protect himself against

---

an obstructing opponent in an attempt to reach a runner. On a punt, field-goal attempt, or Try-kick attempt, a defensive player (B1) may not grab and pull an offensive player out of the way which allows another defensive player(s) (B2) to shoot the gap (pull and shoot) in an attempt to block the kick, unless the defensive player (B1) is advancing towards the kicker.

Exception 1: An eligible receiver is considered to be an obstructing opponent only to a point five yards beyond the line of scrimmage unless the player who receives the snap demonstrates no further intention to pass the ball (including handing off the ball, pitching the ball, or moving out of the pocket). Within this five-yard zone, a defensive player may chuck an eligible receiver in front of him. The defender is allowed to maintain continuous and unbroken contact within the five-yard zone, so long as the receiver has not moved beyond a point that is even with the defender.

Within the five-yard zone, a defender may not make original contact in the back of a receiver, nor may he use his hands or arms to hang on to or encircle a receiver. The defender cannot extend an arm(s) to cut off or hook a receiver causing contact that impedes and restricts the receiver as the play develops, nor may he maintain contact after the receiver has moved beyond a point that is even with the defender.

Beyond the five-yard zone, if the player who receives the snap remains in the pocket with the ball, a defender may use his hands or arms only to defend or protect himself against impending contact caused by a receiver. If the receiver attempts to evade the defender, the defender cannot chuck him, or extend an arm(s) to cut off or hook him, causing contact that re-directs, restricts, or impedes the receiver in any way.

Beyond the five-yard zone, incidental contact may exist between receiver and defender as long as it does not materially affect or significantly impede the receiver, creating a distinct advantage.

Exception 2: Eligible receivers lined up within two yards of the tackle, whether on or behind the line, may be blocked below the waist at or behind the line of scrimmage. No eligible receiver can be blocked below the waist after he goes beyond the line. (Illegal Cut.)

Note 1: Once the quarterback or receiver of the snap hands off, is tackled, pitches the ball to a back, or if the quarterback leaves the pocket area (see 3-24), the restrictions on the defensive team relative to offensive receivers (illegal contact, illegal cut) will end, provided the ball is not in the air.

Note 2: Whenever a team presents an apparent punting formation, defensive action that would normally constitute illegal contact (chuck beyond five yards) will no longer be considered a foul.

Penalty: For illegal contact, illegal cut, or holding by the defense: Loss of five yards and automatic first down.

■ Supplemental Notes

(1) An eligible pass receiver who takes a position more than two yards outside of his own tackle (flexed receiver) may not be blocked below the waist (illegal cut), unless the quarterback hands off, is tackled, pitches the ball to a back, or if the quarterback leaves the pocket area.

(2) The unnecessary use of the hands by the defense, except as provided in Article 4, is illegal and is commonly used in lieu of a legal block (Article 5) (See 12-2-2, 3).

(3) Any offensive player who pretends to possess the ball and/or one to whom a teammate pretends to give the ball, may be tackled provided he is crossing his scrimmage line between the offensive ends of a normal tight offensive line.

Article 7   No defensive player may trip an opponent.

Penalty: For tripping by defense: Loss of 10 yards.

Article 8   A player may not bat or punch:

(a) a loose ball (in field of play) toward opponent's goal line;

(b) a loose ball in any direction if it is in either end zone;

(c) a backward pass in flight may not be batted forward by an offensive player.

Exception: A forward pass in flight may be tipped, batted, or deflected in any direction by any eligible player at any time.

Penalty: For illegal batting or punching the ball: Loss of 10 yards. For enforcement, treat as a foul during a backward pass or fumble (see 8-4-4).

Article 9   No player may deliberately kick any loose ball or ball in player's possession.

Penalty: For illegally kicking the ball: Loss of 10 yards. For enforcement, treat as a foul during a backward pass or fumble (see 8-4-4).

■ Supplemental Notes

(1) If a loose ball is touched by any part of a player's leg (including knee), it is not considered kicking and is treated merely as touching.

(2) If the penalty for an illegal bat or kick is declined, the procedure is the same as though the ball had

been merely muffed. However, if the act (impetus) sends the ball in touch, 3-14-3 applies.

(3) The penalty for Article 6 and 7 does not preclude a penalty for a palpably unfair act, when a deliberate kick or illegal bat actually prevents an opponent from recovering. See Palpably Unfair Act 12-2-3.

(4) The ball is not dead when an illegal kick is recovered.

(5) The illegal kick or bat of a ball in player possession is treated as a foul during fumble (8-4-4).

Section 2   **PERSONAL FOULS**

Article 1   All players are prohibited from:

(a) striking with the fists;

(b) kicking or kneeing;

(c) striking, swinging, or clubbing to the head, neck, or face with the heel, back, or side of the hand, wrist, arm, elbow, or clasped hands (See 12-2-3); or

(d) grabbing the inside collar of the back of the shoulder pads or jersey, or the inside collar of the side of the shoulder pads or jersey, and immediately pulling down the runner. This does not apply to a runner who is in the tackle box or to a quarterback who is in the pocket.

Note: It also is illegal for an opponent to club the passer's arm.

Penalty: For fouls in a, b, c, and d: Loss of 15 yards. If any of the above acts are judged by the official(s) to be flagrant, the offender may be disqualified as long as the entire action is observed by the official(s).

Article 2   A defensive player shall not contact an opponent above the shoulders with the palm of his hands except to ward him off on the line. The exception applies only if it is not a repeated act against the same opponent during any one contact.

Article 3   A defensive player may use the palm of his hands on an opponent's head, neck, or face only to ward off or push him in an actual attempt to get at a loose ball.

Article 4   A player in blocking shall not strike an opponent below the shoulders with his forearm or elbows by turning the trunk of his body at the waist, pivoting, or in any other way that is clearly unnecessary.

Penalty: For illegal use of the palm of the hands or for striking an opponent below the shoulders with the forearm or elbow: Loss of 15 yards.

Note: Any impermissible use of elbows, forearms, or knees shall be penalized under the unnecessary roughness rule; flagrantly unnecessary roughness shall be penalized under the same rule and the player disqualified.

Article 5   No player shall grasp the face mask of an opponent.

Penalty: Incidental grasping of the mask—five yards. Not a personal foul (if by the defense there is no automatic first down). Twisting, turning, or pulling the mask—15 yards. A personal foul. The player may be disqualified if the action is judged by the official(s) to be of a flagrant nature.

Article 6   No defensive player may run into or rough a kicker who kicks from behind his line unless such contact:

(a) is incidental to and after he has touched the kick in flight;

(b) is caused by the kicker's own motions;

(c) occurs during a quick kick;

(d) occurs during a kick or after a run behind the line;

(e) occurs after the kicker recovers a loose ball on the ground; or

(f) is caused because a defender is blocked into the kicker.

Penalty: For running into the kicker: Loss of five yards from the previous spot, no automatic first down. (This is not a personal foul). For roughing the kicker or holder, loss of 15 yards from the previous spot. (This is a personal foul, and also disqualification if flagrant).

■ Supplemental Notes

(1) Avoiding the kicker is a primary responsibility of defensive players if they do not touch the kick.

(2) Any contact with the kicker by a single defensive player who has not touched the kick is running into the kicker.

(3) Any unnecessary roughness committed by defensive players is roughing the kicker. Severity of contact and potential for injury are to be considered.

(4) When two defensive players are making a bona fide attempt to block a kick from scrimmage (punt, drop kick, and/or placekick) and one of them runs into the kicker after the kick has left the kicker's foot at the same instant the second player blocks the kick, the foul for running into the kicker shall not be enforced, unless in the judgment of the Referee, the player running into the kicker was clearly the direct cause of the kick being blocked.

(5) If in the judgment of the Referee any of the above action is unnecessary roughness, the penalty for roughing the kicker shall be enforced from the previous spot as a foul during a kick.

Article 7 There shall be no piling on (3-22).

Penalty: For piling on: Loss of 15 yards.

Note: An official should prevent piling on a prostrate or helpless runner before the ball is dead. When opponents in close proximity to such a runner are about to pile on, and further advance is improbable, the official covering should sound his whistle for a dead ball, in order to prevent further play and roughness. See 7-4-1-d.

Article 8   There shall be no unnecessary roughness. This shall include, but will not be limited to:

(a) striking an opponent anywhere above the knee with the foot or any part of the leg below the knee with a whipping motion;

(b) tackling the runner when he is clearly out of bounds;

(c) a member of the receiving team cannot go out of bounds and contact a kicking team player out of bounds. If this occurs on a kick from scrimmage, post-possession rules would apply if appropriate (9-1-17);

(d) running or diving into, or throwing the body against or on a ball carrier who falls or slips to the ground untouched and makes no attempt to advance, before or after the ball is dead;

(e) unnecessarily running, diving into, cutting, or throwing the body against or on a player who (i) is out of the play or (ii) should not have reasonably anticipated such contact by an opponent, before or after the ball is dead; or throwing the runner to the ground after the ball is dead;

(f) contacting a runner out of bounds. Defensive players must make an effort to avoid contact. Players on defense are responsible for knowing when a runner has crossed the boundary line, except in doubtful cases where he might step on a boundary line and continue parallel with it;

(g) using any part of a player's helmet (including the top/crown and forehead/"hairline" parts) or facemask to butt, spear, or ram an opponent violently or unnecessarily; although such violent or unnecessary use of the helmet and facemask is impermissible against any opponent, game officials will give special attention in administering this rule to protecting those players who are in virtually defenseless postures (e.g., a player in the act of or just after throwing a pass, a receiver catching or attempting to catch a pass, a runner already in the grasp of a tackler, a kickoff or punt returner attempting to field a kick in the air, or a player on the ground at the end of a play). All players in virtually defenseless postures are protected by the same prohibitions against use of the helmet and facemask that are described in the roughing-the-passer rules (see 12-2-12-3);

(h) a kicker/punter, who is standing still or fading backwards after the ball has been kicked, is out of the play and must not be unnecessarily contacted by the receiving team through the end of the play or until he assumes a distinctly defensive position. An opponent may not unnecessarily initiate helmet-to-helmet contact to the kicker/punter during the kick or during the return.

(i) any player who hooks his fingers under the helmet of an opponent and forcibly twists his head.

Penalty: For unnecessary roughness: Loss of 15 yards. The player may be disqualified if the action is judged by the official(s) to be flagrant.

Note: If in doubt about a roughness call or potentially dangerous tactics, the covering official(s) should always call unnecessary roughness.

Article 9   There shall be no clipping from behind and below the waist against a non-runner. This does not apply to

offensive blocking in close-line play where it is legal to
clip above the knee(s), but it is illegal to clip at or below
the knee(s).

Penalty: For clipping: Loss of 15 yards.

■ Supplemental Notes

(1) Close-line play is that which occurs in an area
extending laterally to the position originally occupied
by the offensive tackles and longitudinally three
yards on either side of each line of scrimmage.

(2) In close-line play, if an offensive player's block
(legal or illegal) is followed by the blocker rolling
up on the back of the leg(s) of the defender, the
action is illegal and is considered unnecessary
roughness.

Exception: An offensive lineman may not clip a
defender who, at the snap, is aligned on the line of
scrimmage opposite another offensive lineman who is
more than one position away when the defender is
responding to the flow of the ball away from the
blocker.

Example: Tackle cannot clip nose tackle on sweep away.

(3) Doubtful cases involving a side block or the opponent turning his back as the block is being made are
to be judged according to whether the opponent was
able to see or ward off the blocker.

(4) The use of hands from behind and above the waist
on a non-runner is illegal use of hands.

(5) The use of hands on the back is not a foul when it is
by:

a) one of the kickers in warding off a receiver, while
going downfield under a kick, or

b) any player in an actual personal legal attempt to
recover a loose ball.

(6) It is not considered clipping if:

    a) a blocker is moving in the same direction as an opponent, and has initial contact on the side of the opponent and then continues to contact with the opponent below his waist from behind with any part of his body, or

    b) in any case if an official has not observed the blocker's initial contact.

Article 10   At the snap, an offensive player who is aligned in a position more than two yards laterally outside an offensive tackle, or a player who is in a backfield position at the snap and then moves to a position more than two yards laterally outside a tackle, may not clip an opponent anywhere, nor may he contact an opponent below the waist if the blocker is moving toward the position where the ball was snapped from, and the contact occurs within an area five yards on either side of the line of scrimmage.

Note 1: A player aligned more than two yards laterally outside a tackle at the snap is designated as being flexed.

Note 2: If runner (passer) scrambles on the play, significantly changing the original direction (broken play), the crackback block is legal.

Penalty: Illegal crackback block: Loss of 15 yards.

Article 11   When a player who is aligned in the tackle box at the snap moves to a position outside the box, he cannot initiate contact on the side and below the waist on an opponent if:

a) the blocker is moving toward his own end line; and

b) he approaches the opponent from behind or from the side.

Note: If the near shoulder of the blocker contacts the front of his opponent's body, the "peel back" block is legal.

Penalty: For illegal "peel back" block: Loss of 15 yards.

Article 12   Because the act of passing often puts the quarterback (or any other player attempting a pass) in a position where he is particularly vulnerable to injury, special rules against roughing the passer apply. The Referee has principal responsibility for enforcing these rules. Any physical acts against passers during or just after a pass which, in the Referee's judgment, are unwarranted by the circumstances of the play will be called as fouls. The Referee will be guided by the following principles:

(1) Roughing will be called if, in the Referee's judgment, a pass rusher clearly should have known that the ball had already left the passer's hand before contact was made; pass rushers are responsible for being aware of the position of the ball in passing situations; the Referee will use the release of the ball from the passer's hand as his guideline that the passer is now fully protected; once a pass has been released by a passer, a rushing defender may make direct contact with the passer only up through the rusher's first step after such release (prior to second step hitting the ground); thereafter the rusher must be making an attempt to avoid contact and must not continue to "drive through" or otherwise forcibly contact the passer; incidental or inadvertent contact by a player who is easing up or being blocked into the passer will not be considered significant.

(2) A rushing defender is prohibited from committing such intimidating and punishing acts as "stuffing" a passer into the ground or unnecessarily wrestling or driving him down after the passer has thrown the ball, even if the rusher makes his initial contact with the passer within the one-step limitation provided for in (1) above. When tackling a passer who is in a virtually defenseless posture (e.g., during or just after

throwing a pass), a defensive player must not unnecessarily or violently throw him down and land on top of him with all or most of the defender's weight. Instead, the defensive player must strive to wrap up or cradle the passer with the defensive player's arms.

(3) In covering the passer position, Referees will be particularly alert to fouls in which defenders impermissibly use the helmet and/or facemask to hit the passer, or use hands, arms, or other parts of the body to hit the passer in the head, neck, or face (see also the other unnecessary-roughness rules covering these subjects). A defensive player must not use his facemask or other part of his helmet against a passer who is in a virtually defenseless posture—for example, (a) forcibly hitting the passer's head, neck, or face with the helmet or facemask, regardless of whether the defensive player also uses his arms to tackle the passer by encircling or grasping him, or (b) lowering the head and violently or unnecessarily making forcible contact with the "hairline" or forehead part of the helmet against any part of the passer's body. This rule does not prohibit incidental contact by the mask or non-crown parts of the helmet in the course of a conventional tackle on a passer. A defensive player must not "launch" himself (spring forward and upward) into a passer, or otherwise strike him in a way that causes the defensive player's helmet or facemask to forcibly strike the passer's head, neck, or face—even if the initial contact of the defender's helmet or facemask is lower than the passer's neck. Examples: (a) a defender buries his facemask into a passer's high chest area, but the defender's trajectory as he leaps into the passer causes the defender's helmet to strike the passer violently in the head or face; (b) a defender, using a face-on posture or with

head slightly lowered, hits a passer in an area below the passer's neck, then the defender's head moves upward, resulting in strong contact by the defender's mask or helmet with the passer's head, neck, or face (one example of this is the so-called "dip-and-rip" technique).

(4) A defensive player is prohibited from clubbing the arm of a passer during a pass or just after a pass has been thrown; however, a defensive player may grasp, pull, or otherwise make normal contact with a passer's arm in attempting to tackle him;

(5) A rushing defender is prohibited from forcibly hitting, in the knee area or below, a passer who has one or both feet on the ground, even if the initial contact is above the knee. It is not a foul if the defender is blocked (or fouled) into the passer and has no opportunity to avoid him;

(6) The Referee must blow the play dead as soon as the passer is clearly in the grasp and control of any tackler behind the line, and the passer's safety is in jeopardy;

(7) A passer who is standing still or fading backwards after the ball has left his hand is obviously out of the play and must not be unnecessarily contacted by the defense through the end of the play or until the passer becomes a blocker, or until he becomes a runner upon taking a lateral from a teammate or picking up a loose ball, or, in the event of a change of possession on the play, until the passer assumes a distinctly defensive position. An opponent may not unnecessarily initiate helmet-to-helmet contact to the quarterback at any time after the possession changes.

(8) When the passer goes outside the pocket area and either continues moving with the ball (without

attempting to advance the ball as a runner) or throws while on the run, he loses the protection of the one-step rule provided for in (1) above, but he remains covered by all the other special protections afforded to a passer in the pocket (Numbers 2, 3, 4, 5, 6, and 7), as well as the regular unnecessary-roughness rules applicable to all player positions. If the passer stops behind the line and clearly establishes a passing posture, he will then be covered by all of the special protections for passers.

Penalty: For Roughing the Passer: Loss of 15 yards from the previous spot; disqualification if flagrant.

Note 1: If in doubt about a roughness call or potentially dangerous tactic on the quarterback, the Referee should always call roughing the passer.

Note 2: See 8-3-3 for personal fouls prior to completion or interception.

Article 13   Players on the receiving team are prohibited from blocking below the waist during a down in which there is a kickoff, safety kick, punt, field-goal attempt, or Try-kick.

Exception: Only immediately at the snap on a punt, field-goal attempt, or Try-kick, those defensive players on the line of scrimmage lined up on or inside the normal tight-end position can block low.

All players on the kicking team are prohibited from blocking below the waist after a kickoff, safety kick, punt, field-goal attempt, or Try-kick. After a change of possession, neither team may block below the waist.

Penalty: Loss of 15 yards.

Article 14   A player may not use a helmet (that is no longer worn by anyone) as a weapon to strike, swing at, or throw at an opponent.

Penalty: For illegal use of helmet as a weapon: Loss of 15 yards and automatic disqualification.

Article 15   A chop block is a foul by the offense in which one offense player (designated as A1 for purposes of this rule) blocks a defensive player in the area of the thigh or lower while another offensive player (A2) occupies that same defensive player in one of the circumstances described in sub-sections (1) through (10) below.

(1) On a forward-pass play, A1 chops a defensive player while the defensive player is physically engaged by the blocking attempt of A2.

(2) On a forward-pass play in which A2 physically engages a defensive player with a blocking attempt, A1 chops the defensive player after the contact by A2 has been broken and while A2 is still confronting the defensive player.

(3) On a forward-pass play, A1 chops a defensive player while A2 confronts the defensive player in a pass-blocking posture but is not physically engaged with the defensive player (a "lure").

(4) On a forward-pass play, A1 blocks a defensive player in the area of the thigh or lower, and A2, simultaneously or immediately after the block by A1, engages the defensive player high.

Note: Each of the above circumstances in sub-sections (1) through (4), which describes a chop-block foul on a forward-pass play, also applies on a play in which an offensive player indicates an apparent attempt to pass block but the play ultimately becomes a run.

(5) On a running play, A1 is lined up in the backfield at the snap and subsequently chops a defensive player engaged above the waist by A2, and such block occurs on or behind the line of scrimmage in an area

extending laterally to the positions originally occupied by the tight end on either side.

(6) On a running play, A1, an offensive lineman, chops a defensive player after the defensive player has been engaged by A2 (high or low), and the initial alignment of A2 is more than one position away from A1. This rule applies only when the block occurs at a time when the flow of the play is clearly away from A1.

(7) On a kicking play, A1 chops a defensive player while the defensive player is physically engaged by the blocking attempt of A2.

(8) On a kicking play in which A2 physically engages a defensive player with a blocking attempt, A1 chops the defensive player after the contact by A2 has been broken and while A2 is still confronting the defensive player.

(9) On a kicking play, A1 chops a defensive player while A2 confronts the defensive player in a kick-blocking posture but is not physically engaged with the defensive player (a "lure").

(10) On a kicking play, A1 blocks a defensive player in the area of the thigh or lower, and A2, simultaneously or immediately after the block by A1, engages the defensive player high.

Note: Each of the above circumstances in subsections (7) through (10), which describes a chop-block foul on a kicking play, also applies on a play in which an offensive player indicates an apparent attempt to kick protect, but the play ultimately becomes a run.

Penalty: For Chop Block: Loss of 15 yards.

Section 3 UNSPORTSMANLIKE CONDUCT

Article 1 There shall be no unsportsmanlike conduct. This applies to any act which is contrary to the generally understood principles of sportsmanship. Such acts specifically include, among others:

(a) Throwing a punch, or a forearm, or kicking at an opponent even though no contact is made.

(b) The use of abusive, threatening, or insulting language or gestures to opponents, teammates, officials, or representatives of the League.

(c) The use of baiting or taunting acts or words that engender ill will between teams.

(d) <u>Individual players involved in prolonged or excessive celebrations. Players are prohibited from engaging in any celebrations while on the ground. A celebration shall be deemed excessive or prolonged if a player continues to celebrate after a warning from an official.</u>

(e) Two or more players engage in prolonged, excessive, premeditated, or choreographed celebrations.

(f) <u>Possession or use of foreign or extraneous object(s) that are not part of the uniform during the game on the field or the sideline, or using the ball as a prop.</u>

(g) Unnecessary physical contact with a game official.

(h) Removal by a player of his helmet during or after a play. (Exceptions: The player is not in the game or he is in or has returned to his bench area; or, the player is in the game and a time out has been called for reasons of injury, television break, charged team time out, or it is between periods.

Note 1: Under no condition is an official to allow a player to shove, push, or strike him in an offensive, disrespectful, or unsportsmanlike manner. Any such action must be reported to the Commissioner.

Penalty: (a), (b), (c), (d), (e), (f), and (g): Loss of 15 yards from succeeding spot or whatever spot the Referee, after consulting with the crew, deems equitable.

Note 2: Violations of (b) or (c) (above), which occur before or during the game may result in disqualification in addition to the yardage penalty. Any violations at the game site on the day of the game, including postgame, may result in discipline by the Commissioner. Any violation of (g) (above) may result in disqualification and also will include discipline by the Commissioner. An official must see the entire action for a player to be disqualified.

*Note 3: Violations of (b) will be penalized if any of the acts are committed **directly at an opponent**. These acts include but are not limited to: sack dances; home run swing; incredible hulk; spiking the ball; spinning the ball; throwing or shoving the ball; pointing; pointing the ball; verbal taunting; military salute; standing over an opponent (prolonged and with provocation); or dancing.*

*Note 4: Violations of (c) will be penalized if any of the acts occur **anywhere on the field**. These acts include but are not limited to: throat slash; machine gun salute; sexually suggestive gestures; prolonged gyrations; or stomping on a team logo.*

Note 5: Violations of (d) will be penalized if they occur anywhere on the field other than the bench area.

Note 6: If any foreign object(s) are deemed a safety hazard by the game officials, in addition to a yardage penalty, the player will be subject to ejection from the game, whether he uses the object or not.

(i) The defensive use of acts or words designed to disconcert an offensive team at the snap. An official must blow his whistle immediately to stop play.

(j) Concealing a ball underneath the clothing or using any article of equipment to simulate a ball.

(k) Using entering substitutes, legally returning players, substitutes on sidelines, or withdrawn players to confuse opponents. The clarification is also to be interpreted as covering any lingering by players leaving the field when being substituted for. See 5-2-1.

(l) An offensive player lines up or is in motion less than five yards from the sideline in front of his team's designated bench area. However, an offensive player can line up less than five yards from the sidelines on the same side as his team's player bench, as long as he is not in front of the designated bench area.

(m) Repeatedly abusing the substitution rule (time in) in attempts to conserve time. See 5-2-2.

(n) More than two successive 40/25 second penalties (after warning) during same down.

(o) Jumping or standing on a teammate or opponent to block or attempt to block an opponent's kick.

(p) Placing a hand or hands on a teammate or opponent to gain additional height in the block or attempt to block an opponent's kick.

(q) Being picked up by a teammate in a block or an attempt to block an opponent's kick.

(r) Clearly running forward and leaping in an obvious attempt to block a field goal or Try-kick after touchdown and landing on players, unless the leaping player was originally lined up within one yard of the line of scrimmage when the ball was snapped.

(s) Goal-tending by a defensive player leaping up to deflect a kick as it passes above the crossbar of a goalpost is prohibited. The Referee could award three points for a palpably unfair act (12-3-3).

(t) A punter, placekicker, or holder who simulates being roughed or run into by a defensive player.

(u) A member of the kicking team who goes out of bounds, whether forced out or voluntarily, must attempt to return inbounds in a reasonable amount of time.

    (v) An attempt to call an excess or illegal time out to freeze a kicker prior to a field-goal attempt or a Try attempt, when:

       (i) a team has already been charged a time out during the same dead-ball period; or

       (ii) a team has exhausted the three charged team time outs that are permitted in a half.

If an attempt is made to call a time out in these situations, the officials shall not grant a time out, play will continue, and a penalty for unsportsmanlike conduct shall be enforced. If a time out is inadvertently granted, the penalty shall also be enforced.

Note: The Referee (or another official) will notify the Head Coach (i) that two charged time outs by the same team in the same dead-ball period are not permitted, and (ii) when he has exhausted his three charged team time outs in a half.

Penalty: For unsportsmanlike player conduct (g) through (v): Loss of 15 yards from:

a) **the succeeding spot if the ball is dead.**

b) **the previous spot if the ball was in play.**

If the infraction is flagrant, the player is also disqualified.

Article 2   The defense shall not commit successive or continued fouls to prevent a score.

Penalty: For continuous fouls to prevent a score: If the violation is repeated after a warning, the score involved is awarded to the offensive team.

Article 3   A player or substitute shall not interfere with play by any act which is palpably unfair.

Penalty: For a palpably unfair act: Offender may be disqualified. The Referee, after consulting his crew, enforces any such distance penalty as they consider equitable and irrespective of any other specified code penalty. The Referee could award a score. See 15-1-6.

Non-Player Conduct

Rule 13

Non-Player Conduct

Section 1 **NON-PLAYER CONDUCT**

Article 1 There shall be no unsportsmanlike conduct by a substitute, coach, attendant, or any other non-player (entitled to sit on a team's bench) during any period or time out (including between halves).

■ **Supplemental Notes**

(1) "Loudspeaker" coaching from the sidelines is not permissible.
(2) A player may communicate with a coach provided the coach is in his prescribed area during dead-ball periods.

Article 2 Either or both team attendants and their helpers may enter the field to attend their team during a team time out by either team. No other non-player may come on the field without the Referee's permission, unless he is an incoming substitute (5-2-1).

Article 3 With the exception of uniformed players eligible to participate in the game, all persons in a team's bench area must wear a visible credential clearly marked "BENCH." For all NFL games—preseason, regular-season, and postseason—the home club will be issued a maximum of 27 credentials and the visiting club will be issued a maximum of 25 credentials for use in its bench area. Such credentials must be worn by coaches, players under contract to the applicable club but ineligible to participate in the game, and team support personnel (trainers, doctors, equipment men). From time to time, persons with game-services credentials (e.g., oxygen technicians, ball boys) and authorized club personnel not regularly assigned to the bench area may be in a team's bench area for a brief period without bench credentials. Clubs are prohibited from allowing into their bench areas any persons who are not officially affiliated with the club or otherwise serving a necessary game-day function.

Article 4   All team personnel must observe the zone restrictions applicable to the bench area and the border rimming the playing field. The only persons permitted within the solid six-foot white border (1-1) while play is in progress on the field are game officials. For reasons involving the safety of participating players whose actions may carry them out of bounds, officials' unobstructed coverage of the game, and spectators' sightlines to the field, the border rules must be observed by all coaches and players in the bench area. Violators are subject to penalty by the officials.

Article 5   Coaches and other non-participating team personnel (including uniformed players not in the game at the time) are prohibited from moving laterally along the sidelines any further than the points that are 18 yards from the middle of the bench area (i.e., 32-yard lines to left and right of bench areas when benches are placed on opposite sides of the field). Lateral movement within the bench area must be behind the solid six-foot white border (see Article 4 above).

Article 6   Clubs are prohibited from allowing into the non-bench areas of field level any persons who have not been accredited to those locations by the home club's public-relations office for purposes related to news-media coverage, stadium operations, or pregame and halftime entertainment. The home club is responsible for keeping the field level cleared of all unauthorized persons. Photographers and other personnel accredited for field-level work must not be permitted in the end zones or any other part of the official playing field while play is in progress.

Penalty: For illegal acts under Articles 1 through 6 above: Loss of 15 yards from team for whose supposed benefit foul was made. (Unsportsmanlike conduct.)

Enforcement is from:

a) succeeding spot if the ball is dead.
b) whatever spot the Referee, after consulting with crew, deems equitable, if the ball was in play.

For a flagrant violation, the Referee may exclude offender or offenders from the playing field enclosure for the remainder of the game.

Note: See 4-1-4-Note, for a foul by non-players between halves.

Article 7   A non-player shall not commit any act which is palpably unfair.

Penalty: For a palpably unfair act, see 12-3-3. The Referee, after consulting the crew, shall make such ruling as they consider equitable (15-1-6 and Note) (unsportsmanlike conduct).

Note: Various actions involving a palpably unfair act may arise during a game. In such cases, the officials may award a distance penalty in accordance with 12-3-3, even when it does not involve disqualification of a player or substitute. See 17-1.

Article 8   Non-player personnel of a club (e.g., management personnel, coaches, trainers, equipment men) are prohibited from making unnecessary physical contact with or directing abusive, threatening, or insulting language or gestures at opponents, game officials, or representatives of the League.

Penalty: Loss of 15 yards. (Unsportsmanline conduct.) Enforcement is from:

a) succeeding spot if the ball is dead;

b) previous spot if the ball was in play; or
c) whatever spot the Referee, after consulting with the crew, deems equitable. (Palpably Unfair Act.)

Note: Violations which occur before or during the game may result in disqualification in addition to the yardage penalty. Any violation at the game site on the day of the game, including postgame, may result in discipline by the Commissioner.

Penalty Enforcement

Rule 14

Penalty Enforcement

(Governing all cases not otherwise specifically provided for)

Section 1 **SPOT FROM WHICH PENALTY IN FOUL IS ENFORCED**

Article 1 The general provisions of Rule 14 govern all spots of enforcement.

Note: The spot of enforcement for fouls by players or the actual distance penalty or both, when not specific, are subordinate to the specific rules governing a foul during a fumble, pass, or kick. These in turn are both subordinate to Rule 14.

Article 2 When a foul by a player occurs between downs, enforcement is from the succeeding spot (14-5-S.N. 3).

Article 3 Penalties for fouls committed by non-players shall be enforced as specifically provided under Rule 13.

Article 4 When the spot of enforcement is not governed by a general or specific rule, it is the spot of the foul.

Article 5 The basic spots of enforcement (3-11-1) are:

(a) The previous spot for a forward pass (8-3-2); a scrimmage kick (9-1-17); or a free kick (6-2-5).
(b) The dead ball spot on a running play (14-1-12).
(c) The spot of snap, backward pass, or fumble (8-4-4).
(d) The spot of the foul (14-1-4 and 14-1-13).
(e) The succeeding spot for dead-ball fouls. When such a foul by the defense incurs a penalty that results in the offensive team being short of the previous spot, the ball will be advanced to the previous spot.

Note: If a foul is committed during a run, a fumble, or a backward pass, the penalty is assessed from the basic spot if:

i)   Defense fouls in advance of the basic spot

> ii) *Defense fouls behind the basic spot*
> iii) *Offense fouls in advance of the basic spot*

If the offense fouls behind the basic spot, enforcement is from the spot of the foul (3 and 1).

Exceptions:

1) All fouls committed by the offensive team behind the line of scrimmage (except in the end zone) shall be penalized from the previous spot. If the foul is in the end zone, it is a safety (14-1-11-b).

2) If a runner (3-27-1) is downed behind the line of scrimmage (except in the end zone) and the foul by an offensive player is beyond the line of scrimmage, enforcement shall be from the previous spot. If the runner is down in the end zone, it is a safety (11-4-1-a).

Article 6   When the spot of a player foul is out of bounds between the end lines, it is assumed to be at an inbounds line on a yard line (extended) through the spot where the foul was committed. If this spot is behind an end line, it is assumed to be in the end zone. See 7-3-7 and 14-1-11.

Article 7   A dead-ball foul is enforced from the succeeding spot, and the down counts.

Article 8   Dead-ball fouls by both teams are offset at the succeeding spot and the down counts, except when one or both are disqualifying fouls, or as provided in 14-1-9. See 14-3-2.

Article 9   If there has been a foul by either team during a down and there is a dead-ball foul by the other team in the action immediately after the end of the down, it is a double foul, and all rules for enforcement of double fouls apply (see 14-3-1).

Exception: If the scoring team commits a dead-ball foul after a score, the down counts, and the penalty is enforced on the kickoff.

Article 10   There is no penalty unless the contact was avoidable and it is deemed unnecessary roughness, if a player:

(a) uses his hands, arms, or body in a manner ordinarily illegal (other than striking) during the dead-ball period after a down ends, or

(b) completes a legal action (blocking or tackling) started during the down.

Article 11   When a spot of enforcement is behind the offensive goal line, and the foul is:

(a) by the defense, a distance penalty is measured from the goal line (unless a touchback, one during a backward pass, or fumble, or 12-1-4-Penalty Exception), or

(b) by the offense, it is a safety. See 8-4-4 for exception.

Note: During a loose ball there is always an offensive and defensive team, and enforcement is provided for in the specific section governing passes, fumbles, and kicks. See 3-2-3; 3-16; 3-35-1; and 14-1-5.

Article 12   When a foul occurs during a running play (3-27-2) and the run in which the foul occurs is not followed by a change of team possession during the down, the spot of enforcement is the spot where the ball is dead.

Exceptions:

1) When the spot of a foul by the offense is behind the spot where dead, enforcement is from the spot of the foul.

2) When the spot of a foul by the offense is behind the line of scrimmage, enforcement is from the previous spot unless in offensive's end zone. Then it is a safety (14-1-11-b).

3) When the spot of a foul by the offense is beyond the line of scrimmage and a runner (3-27-1) is downed behind the line, enforcement is from the previous

spot unless he is downed in the end zone. Then it is a safety, the result of the play (11-4-1).

4) When the spot of foul is that of an illegal forward pass, enforcement is from the spot of the foul. This does not apply to a second forward pass from behind the line, or a pass after the ball had gone beyond the line, which is enforced from the previous spot.

5) If the spot of a defensive foul occurs on or beyond the line of scrimmage and the ball becomes dead behind the line, penalty is enforced from the previous spot.

6) When the spot of enforcement for the defense is behind the offensive goal line, enforcement is from the goal line. See 14-1-11-a.

7) When the spot of a foul by the defense is behind the line of scrimmage and the ball becomes dead behind the line, enforcement is from the spot of the foul or the spot where the ball is dead, whichever is more advantageous to the offense. If such foul incurs a penalty that results in the offended team being short of the line, the ball will be advanced to the previous spot and no additional yardage assessed.

Article 13 When a defensive foul occurs during a running play (3-27-2) and the run in which the foul occurs is followed by a change of possession, the spot of enforcement is the spot of the foul and ball reverts to offensive team. See 14-1-12- Exc. 5.

Exceptions:

1) When the spot of a foul is in advance of the spot where the offensive player lost possession, the spot of enforcement is the spot where player possession was lost and the ball reverts to offensive team.

2) When the spot of a foul by the defense is at, behind, or beyond the line of scrimmage, and such foul incurs a penalty that results in the offensive team

being short of the line, the ball will be advanced to the previous spot.

Note: When there are multiple fouls by the defense, enforcement should benefit the offense the most.

■ Supplemental Notes

(1) A foul during a run prior to a kick or forward pass from behind the line, is enforced as if it had occurred during a pass or kick which follows. See 8-3-2, 3, 4; 9-1-17; and 14-1-5.

(2) If an offensive player fouls behind the defensive goal line during a running play in which the runner crosses that line, the penalty is enforced from the spot where the runner crossed the goal line. See 7-3-7.

(3) After a penalty for a foul during a running play, the general provisions of 14-8-1 relative to the number of the ensuing down, always apply.

(4) Any foul prior to possession by a runner is enforced as otherwise specified.

Article 14   If a team scores and the opponent commits a personal or unsportsmanlike conduct foul or a palpably unfair act during the down, the penalty is enforced on the succeeding free kick unless the enforcement resulted in the score.

Note: If the personal foul, unsportsmanlike conduct foul, or a palpably unfair act by the opponent occurred on a successful field goal or Try kick, the penalty could be enforced from the previous spot and the offensive team would retain the ball, with no score.

Section 2   LOCATION OF FOUL

Article 1   If a distance penalty, enforced from a specific spot between the goal lines, would place the ball more than half the distance to the offender's goal line, the penalty shall be half the distance from that spot to their goal line.

Note: This general rule supersedes any other general or specific rule other than for a palpably unfair act or the enforcement for intentional grounding, if appropriate.

Article 2

(a) If a foul occurs behind a goal line during a down, the penalty shall be enforced as provided for under the specific running play, pass, or fumble rule involved.

(b) If a foul occurs between downs, enforcement is from the succeeding spot (14-5).

(c) If any enforcement leaves or places the ball behind a goal line, Rule 11, Section 3, 4, and 6, govern. See 14-1-11 and Note.

Section 3   **FOULS BY BOTH TEAMS**

Article 1   If there is a double foul (3-11-2-c) without a change of possession, the penalties are offset and the down is replayed at the previous spot. If it was a scrimmage down, the number of the next down and the necessary line is the same as for the down for which the new one is substituted.

Exceptions:

1) If one of the fouls is of a nature that incurs a 15-yard penalty and the other foul of a double foul normally would result in a loss of 5 yards only (15 yards versus 5 yards), the major penalty yardage is to be assessed from the previous spot.

Note: If a score occurs on a play that would normally involve a 5- vs. 15-yard enforcement, enforce the major penalty from the previous spot.

2) Any disqualified player is removed immediately, even when one or both fouls are disqualifying or are disregarded otherwise. See 14-1-8.

3) If both fouls involve disqualification, the down is replayed at the previous spot. If both fouls are dead-ball fouls or are treated as such (14-1-8), the fouls are disregarded and the ball is next put in play at the succeeding spot. See Exception 1 in either case.

4) If the one foul by the kickers during a down is illegal touching of a scrimmage kick, the down is not replayed at the previous spot. The foul (illegal touching) by the kickers is disregarded provided the distance penalty for a foul by the receivers is enforced. If not enforced, the receivers next put the ball in play at any spot of illegal touching or at any other spot where they are entitled to possession at the end of the down. However, a postpossession foul cannot be declined in order to force B's possession at any spot of illegal touching (9-1-17-Exc. 2).

Note: Any foul by either team after a kick ends is enforced as ordinary. See 9-1-17.

Article 2 If there is a double foul (3-11-2-c) during a down in which there is a change of possession, the team gaining possession must keep the ball after enforcement for its foul, provided its foul occurred after the change of possession (clean hands).

Exceptions:

1) If the kickers foul during a kickoff, punt, safety kick, or field-goal attempt before possession changes, the receivers will have the option of replaying the down at the previous spot (offsetting fouls), or keeping the ball after enforcement for its fouls.

2) If the team gaining possession fouls and loses possession, the penalties are offset and the down is replayed at the previous spot.

3) If a score would result from a foul by a team gaining possession, the down is replayed at the previous spot.

If the team gaining possession fouls prior to the change of possession (not clean hands), the penalties are offset and the down is replayed at the previous spot.

Article 3   If a double foul occurs after a change in possession, the team in possession retains the ball at the spot where the team in possession's foul occurred so long as that spot is not in advance of the dead-ball spot. In that event, ball is spotted at dead-ball spot.

  (a) If this spot is normally a touchback, the ball is placed on the 20-yard line.
  (b) If normally a safety, place the ball on 1-yard line.
  (c) This enforcement also applies if one of the fouls is a postpossession foul.
  (d) If there is a subsequent change of possession (e.g., fumble recovery) after the double foul, and the foul by the team in possession is in advance of the spot of the fumble, the ball is put in play by the fumbling team at the spot of the fumble.
  (e) If the foul by the team in possession is a dead-ball foul, the ball is put in play at the dead-ball spot.

■ Supplemental Notes

  (1) When enforcement for a double foul is disregarded, the number of the next down, if a scrimmage down, is the same as if no foul had occurred. See 14-3-2.
  (2) If there is a foul by the defensive team from the start of a snap until a legal forward pass ends, it is not treated as a double foul except as provided in 8-3-3,4.
  (3) Change of possession refers to the physical change of possession from one team to the other except for kicks from scrimmage (9-1-17), and free kick (4-3-1-Note 3).
  (4) If a team fouls before it gains possession on a double foul, it cannot score.

(5) Illegal touching of a scrimmage kick, while technically a foul, does not offset a foul committed by its opponent. It is not considered part of a double foul. See 14-3-1-Exc. 4.

(6) If there is a dead-ball foul by the defensive team after a legal forward pass becomes incomplete, both penalties are enforced. See 14-1-7.

Section 4 **CHOICE OF PENALTIES**

If there is a multiple foul (3-11-2-b) by the same team during the same down, only one penalty may be enforced after the Referee has explained the alternatives. The captain of the offended team shall make the choice.

Note: A disqualified player is always removed, regardless of any captain's choice. See 5-1-3.

Section 5 **TIME OF FOUL**

If a foul occurs between downs (3-11-2-d), a distance penalty is enforced from the succeeding spot. See 14-1-7 to 10.

■ **Supplemental Notes**

(1) When a foul occurs simultaneously with an out of bounds or after a loose ball crosses the plane of the boundary line in the air and then first touches anything out of bounds, it is considered to be a dead-ball foul.

(2) The succeeding spot for a foul after a touchdown and before a whistle for a Try is the next kickoff (3-11-1-Exc.).

(3) The time between downs is the interval during all time outs (including intermissions) and from the time the ball is dead until it is next put in play (time in). See 3-36-1, 2.

(4) For a dead-ball foul by the defensive team or by either team at the end of a play not from scrimmage, see 14-8-5 and 6.

(5) See 5-1-5-S.N. 2 for a special enforcement between downs.

Section 6 **REFUSAL OF PENALTIES**

Penalties for all fouls, unless otherwise expressly provided for, may be declined by the captain of the offended team, in which case play proceeds as though no foul had been committed.

Note: The yardage distance for any penalty may be declined, even though the penalty is accepted.

Exceptions:

1) A disqualified or suspended player is always removed, even when an accompanying distance penalty is declined, or when a penalty for another foul is chosen (multiple foul).

2) During a down a foul occurs (includes an incomplete forward pass), for which the ball is dead immediately.

3) The penalty for certain illegal actions prior to or pertaining to a snap or to a free kick may not be declined, i.e., the ball remains dead.

   a) 40/25-second violations (4-3-9).

   b) Snap made before the Referee can assume his normal stance (7-3-3-c-2).

4) When a 40/25-second penalty occurs prior to the snap, the defensive team may decline a distance penalty, in which case the down is replayed from the previous spot.

5) If fouls are committed by both teams during the same down (double foul), no penalty may be

declined, except as provided for kickers when their only foul is illegal touching of a scrimmage kick. See 14-3-1-Exc. 4.

6) If the defensive team commits a foul during an unsuccessful Try, the offensive team may decline the distance penalty and the down is replayed from the previous spot.

Section 7   **ON INCOMPLETE FORWARD PASS**

An illegal forward pass is a foul, but an incomplete forward pass is not classed as a foul and the penalties provided therefore may not be declined.

Exception: If a team commits a foul during the same play in which it makes an incomplete forward pass, the captain of the offended team may elect which of the penalties is to be enforced (14-4).

Note: If there is a dead-ball foul by either team after an incompletion, enforcement is from the succeeding spot. See 14-5.

Section 8   **NUMBER OF DOWN AFTER PENALTY**

Article 1   After a distance penalty (not combined with a loss-of-down penalty) for a foul by the offensive team prior to (between downs) or during a play from scrimmage which results in the ball being in its possession behind the necessary line, the number of the ensuing down is the same as that of the down before which or during which the foul occurred.

Article 2   A combination penalty involving both distance and loss-of-down is enforced for certain forward-pass fouls by the offensive team.

Examples:

(a) from beyond the line (8-1-1-Pen., c); or

(b) intentionally grounded (8-3-1).

Note: After a loss-of-down penalty (prior to fourth down), the number of the ensuing down is one greater than that of the previous down. If it occurs on fourth down, it is loss of the ball to the defensive team unless it is a combination penalty, in which case the distance penalty is enforced in addition to the loss of the ball. See 8-1-1-S.N. 4.

Article 3   When a foul occurs during a play from scrimmage, the necessary line remains the same regardless of any change of team possession thereafter.

Article 4   After a distance penalty for a foul by the offensive team during a play from scrimmage which results in the ball being in advance of the necessary line, it is a first-and-10 for the offensive team.

Articles 4 and 6 also apply to a dead-ball foul of the offensive team at the end of a play from scrimmage during which it has been constantly in possession.

Article 5   After a penalty for a foul by the defense prior to (between downs) or during a play from scrimmage, the ensuing down is first-and-10 for the offense.

Exceptions are:

1) offside;
2) encroachment;
3) neutral zone infraction;
4) delay of game;
5) illegal substitution;
6) excess time out;
7) running into kicker;
8) incidental facemask; and
9) more than 11 players on the field at the snap.

In the above nine exceptions the number of the down and the necessary line remain the same unless a distance penalty places the ball on or in advance of that line, in which case it is first-and-10 for A.

Article 6   After a distance penalty for a foul which occurs during a play after team possession has changed following a snap or free kick, it is first-and-10 for the team that was in possession at the time of the foul or at the time of the dead-ball foul.

Article 7   After a loss of ball penalty, it is first-and-10 for the offended team after enforcement, unless the offended team free kicks following the fair-catch interference.

Note: Loss of ball results only from illegal touching of kick (other than a free kick) or a fair-catch interference. See 6-2-4 and 10-1-4.

Officials: Jurisdiction and Duties

Rule 15

Officials: Jurisdiction and Duties

Section 1 OFFICIALS

Article 1   By League action, the officials' manual is an integral part of the official rules, especially in regard to the specific duties, mechanics, and procedures for each official during any play situations. For that reason, many such specific items are omitted in Sections 1 to 8 to avoid needless repetition, and only the primary duties of each official are stated. Some of the technical terms used hereafter are defined only in the manual.

Note: The terms "On Ball" or "Cover" imply that an official is nearest or in close proximity to a loose ball or runner and is in position to declare the ball dead when the down ends by rule. See 15-1-11-S.N. 1-3.

Article 2   The game officials are: Referee, Umpire, Head Linesman, Line Judge, Field Judge, Side Judge, and Back Judge.

Note: In the absence of seven officials, the crew is to be rearranged, on the most feasible basis, according to the other members of crew.

Article 3   All officials are to wear uniforms prescribed by the League (including a black cap with visor and piping for all except the Referee, who will wear a white cap). All officials will carry a whistle and a weighted, bright gold flag.

Article 4   An official is to blow his whistle:

(a) for any foul for which ball remains dead or is dead immediately;

(b) to signal time out at end of a down, during which he has indicated a foul, by means of dropping his flag and provided no other official signalled time out at end of down;

(c) to indicate dead ball when he is covering a runner.
See 7-4-1, 2, 3, 4, 5.

(d) at any other time, when he is nearest to ball, when a
down ends. See 15-8-3.

*Note: The flag is to be used to indicate a foul. See 7-4-5-
Note.*

Article 5 Members of the crew are required to meet in their dressing quarters at least 2 hours and 15 minutes before game time.

Note: By order of the Commissioner, from the time any official first enters the dressing room, and until all officials have left it at the end of the game, no person other than clubhouse attendants or those invited by the Referee shall be allowed to enter it. This prohibition includes coaches, players, owners, and other management personnel.

Article 6 All officials are responsible for any decision involving the application of a rule, its interpretation, or an enforcement. If an official errs in his interpretation of a rule, the other officials must check him before play is resumed, otherwise they are equally responsible. In the event of a disagreement, the crew should draw aside for a conference.

Note: If, because of injury, the officials' vote is tied, Referee's decision will be the deciding factor. Any dissenting opinion is to be reported to the supervisor.

Article 7 All officials have concurrent jurisdiction over any foul, and there is no fixed territorial division in this respect. When an official signals a foul, he must report it to the Referee, informing him of its nature, position of ball at time of foul, the offender (when known), the penalty, and spot of enforcement.

Article 8 Each official is to record every foul he signals and the total number of officials signalling the same foul. During the game, these are to be recorded on game cards provided by the League. They are to be preserved after each game in case they should be needed to revise an official's final game card.

Article 9 At the end of the game the officials are to record their own fouls on game cards provided by the league, and are to check them with other officials, for duplications, before leaving the dressing room.

Note: Game cards are to be made out in accordance with the yearly bulletin issued for that purpose.

Article 10 All members of a crew are equally responsible for any errors in officiating mechanics as prescribed by the manual, and are required to call the attention of this fact to an official who has been remiss.

Note: This applies to such errors, in mechanics or applications of rules, as tend to increase the length of the game (elapsed time), and particularly so to those which result in undue loss of playing time (crew time). In the latter case, if the Referee has clearly failed to signal a Referee's time out as specified by rule, any official should do so. See 4-3-7 and 4-3-9.

Article 11 Ten minutes before the opening kickoff, the entire crew is to appear on the field. Three minutes prior to the kickoff the Referee is to make the toss of the coin. He is to indicate which team is to receive and is to do the same when teams first appear on the field prior to the start of the second half. See 4-2-1 and S.N.

Note: All officials record results of coin toss and options chosen.

■ Supplemental Notes

(1) During any running play (includes runbacks), or a loose ball, the nearest official is to cover and remain

with the ball or runner, unless outdistanced until end of down. In such case any nearer official is to cover. See 15-2-9-Note, for Referee entering a side zone and 15-3-4 for Umpire.

(2) When a ball is dead inbounds near a side line, during time in, the official covering is to use the clock signal to indicate this fact.

(3) Any officials not involved in an enforcement are to see that all players other than captains remain aside during any conference between Referee and captains. See 15-2-5.

Article 12   All officials must record charged team time outs.

Section 2   **REFEREE**

Article 1   The Referee is to have general oversight and control of the game. He is the final authority for the score, and the number of a down in case of a disagreement. His decisions upon all matters not specifically placed under the jurisdiction of other officials, either by rule or the officials' manual, are to be final. See 15-1-6-Note and 15-1-10.

Article 2   Prior to the kickoff to start each half and after every time out, the Referee shall sound his whistle for play to start without asking captains if they are ready. In such cases where time is in with his whistle, he is to indicate it by use of clock signal.

Article 3   He is to see that the ball is properly put in play and shall decide on all matters pertaining to its position and disposition at end of down. If any official sounds his whistle, the ball is dead (7-4-1). In case the Referee is informed or believes that ball was dead before such signal or down ends, he has the authority to make a retroactive ruling after consulting the crew or the official involved.

Article 4   The Referee must notify the coach and field captain when his team has used its three charged time outs, signal both coaches when two minutes remain in a half, and positively inform the coach of any disqualified player. He may not delegate any such notifications to any other person. He will announce on the microphone when each period is ended. See 4-3-8-Exc.

Article 5   After a foul, the Referee (in the presence of both captains) must announce the penalty and explain to the offended captain the decision and choice (if any) as well as number of next down and distance (usually approximate) to necessary line for any possible positions of ball. See 7-1-2. The Referee is to designate the offending player, when known. After an enforcement (7-3-2) he shall signal to spectators the nature of penalty by means of the visual signals specifically provided for herein.

Note: It is not necessary for the Referee to explain to both captains the decision and distance to the necessary line in such cases when the enforcement is entirely automatic and/or when there is obviously no choice.

Field captains only may appeal to Referee, and then solely on questions of interpretation of the rules. They shall not be allowed to question the judgment of jurisdiction of any particular official in regard to a foul or in signalling dead ball.

Article 6   Prior to the snap, the Referee shall assume such a stance that he is in the clear of and behind any backfield player. This is also to be construed as including the normal path of any player in motion behind the line as well as the line of vision between such a player and the maker of a pass (forward or backward). He shall also favor the right side (if the passer is right-handed). He will count offensive players.

Article 7   At the end of any down, the Referee may (when in doubt or at the request of a captain, unless obviously unnecessary) request the linesman and his assistants to bring the yardage chains on field to determine whether the ball has reached the necessary line. See 4-3-10-S.N. 4.

Article 8 Prior to each snap, the Referee is to positively check the number of the ensuing down and distance to be gained with the Linesman, signal the Back Judge when to start his watch for the timing of 25 seconds (when appropriate), and know the eligible pass receivers.

Article 9 He is primarily responsible for spotting the ball at the inbounds spot on plays from scrimmage, and should not enter a side zone to cover a runner (other than the quarterback) when the Linesman or Line Judge is in position to do so. See 15-1-11-S.N. 1.

Note: When the ball is dead near the side line during time in, he is not to assist in a relay to the inbounds spot, unless the umpire has been remiss or delayed in doing so (15-1-10-Note and 15-3-4). In such a case, the Umpire is to spot. See Rule 2-2 and Note, in regard to using a new ball at start of second and fourth periods in case of a wet ball.

Section 3 UMPIRE

Article 1 The Umpire has primary jurisdiction over the equipment and the conduct and actions of players on the scrimmage line.

Article 2 Before the game, the Umpire with assistance of other officials shall inspect the equipment of players. He may order any changes he deems necessary to any proposed equipment which is considered dangerous or confusing (5-3). This authority extends throughout the game.

Article 3 He shall assist in relaying the ball:

(a) to the inbounds spot when it is dead near a side line during time in when feasible (15-2-9-Note);

(b) to the previous spot after an incompletion; and

(c) to the spot of a free kick when indicated. See 15-1-11-S.N.

Article 4   The Umpire shall record:

(a) all charged team time outs during the game;
(b) the winner of the toss; and
(c) the score.

He is to assist the Referee on decisions involving possession of the ball in close proximity to the line, after a loose ball or runner has crossed it. He and the Line Judge are to determine whether ineligible linemen illegally cross the line prior to a pass, and he must wipe a wet ball in accordance with the proper timing. He should count the offensive players on the field at the snap.

Section 4   **LINESMAN**

Article 1   The Linesman operates on the side of field designated by the Referee during the first half and on opposite side during the second half unless ordered otherwise. See 1-4-Note for exception.

Article 2   He is responsible for illegal motion, offside, encroaching, and any actions pertaining to scrimmage line prior to or at snap; and for covering in his side zone. See 15-1-11-S.N. 1; 15-2-9; and 15-3-4. He will count offensive players.

Article 3   Prior to the game, he shall see that his chain crew is properly instructed as to their specific duties and mechanics.

Note: Each home team appoints the official chain crew (boxman, two rodmen and alternate, drive start, and forward stake indicator) subject to approval by the League office. Each member carries a working pass to that effect, and it is prohibited for anyone else to work as such. The standardized yardage chains and downs box must be used, and if any others are furnished, this fact is to be reported to the Commissioner.

Article 4   The Linesman shall use a clamp on the chain when measuring for first down.

Article 5   The Linesman is to mark with his foot (when up with ball) the yard line touched by forward point of ball at end of each scrimmage down. At the start of each new series of downs, he and the rodmen set the yardage chains when the Referee so signals. He positively must check with the Referee as to the number of each down that is about to start.

Note: It is mandatory for Linesman to personally see that rear rod is accurately set and also to see that the forward rodman and boxman have set the safety markers for the forward rod and the previous spot, during any series of downs, as prescribed by the officials' manual.

Article 6   On his own side, he is to assist the Line Judge as to illegal motion or a shift and Umpire in regard to holding or illegal use of hands on end of line (especially during kicks or passes), and know eligible pass receivers.

Article 7   He is to mark out-of-bounds spot on his side of field when within his range and is to supervise substitutions made by team located on his side of field during either half.

Note: See 15-1-11-S.N. 1; 15-2-9; and 15-3-4.

Section 5   **LINE JUDGE**

Article 1   The Line Judge is to operate on side of field opposite the Linesman.

Article 2   He is responsible for the timing of game. He also is responsible for illegal motion, illegal shift, and for covering in his side zone. See 15-1-11-S.N. 1 and 15-2-9. He will count offensive players.

Article 3   He is responsible for supervision of the timing and in case the game clock becomes inoperative, or for any other reason is not being operated correctly, he shall take over the official timing on the field.

Article 4   He is to time each period and (4-1-3, 4), signal the Referee when two minutes remain in a half and leave in ample time with the Field Judge to notify their respective teams of five minutes before the start of the second half.

Article 5   He shall advise the Referee when time has expired at end of a period.

Article 6   He must notify both captains, through the Referee, of the time remaining for play not more than 10 or less than five minutes before the end of each half and must signal Referee when two minutes remain in each half. In the event that the stadium clock is inoperable, he must notify both captains, through the Referee, of the time remaining for play not more than 10 or less than 5 minutes before the end of each half and must signal Referee when two minutes remain in each half.

Note: Upon inquiry of a field captain, he may state the approximate time remaining for play at any time during the game, provided he does not comply with such request more than three times during the last five minutes of either half, and provided it will not affect playing time near the end of a half (4-3-10).

Article 7   On his own side, he is to:

(a) assist the Linesman as to offside or encroaching;
(b) assist the Umpire as to holding or illegal use of hands on the end of the line (especially during kicks or passes);

(c) assist the Referee as to whether a pass is forward or backward behind the line and false starts; and

(d) be responsible for knowing the eligible pass receivers.

Article 8   He is to:

(a) mark the out-of-bounds spot of all plays on his side, when within his range (See 15-1-11-S.N. 1-3 and 15-2-9);

(b) supervise substitutions made by the team seated on his side of the field during either half (see 5-2-1);

(c) notify the home-team head coach with the Field Judge five minutes before the start of the second half.

Section 6   FIELD JUDGE

Article 1   The Field Judge will operate on the same side of the field as the Line Judge, 20 yards deep.

Article 2   The Field Judge shall count the number of defensive players on the field at the snap.

Article 3   He shall be responsible for all eligible receivers on his side of the field.

Article 4   After receivers have cleared line of scrimmage, the Field Judge will concentrate on action in the area between the Umpire and Back Judge.

Article 5   In addition to the specified use of the whistle by all officials (15-1-4), the Field Judge is also to use his whistle when, upon his positive knowledge, he knows:

(a) that ball is dead;

(b) that time is out;

(c) that time is out at the end of a down, during which a foul was signaled by a marker, no whistle has sounded in such cases; and

(d) that even in the presence of a whistle up or down field, he is to sound his whistle when players are some distance from such signal. This will help prevent dead-ball fouls.

Article 6   The Field Judge will assist Referee in decisions involving any catching, recovery, out of bounds spot, or illegal touching of a loose ball after it has crossed the scrimmage line, and particularly so for such actions that are out of the range of the Line Judge and Umpire. See 15-1-11-S.N. 1.

Article 7   On field-goal attempts or Try-kick attempts, the Field Judge will station himself on the end line and cover the upright opposite the Back Judge. He, along with the Back Judge, is responsible for indication to the Referee whether the kick is high enough and through the uprights.

Section 7   **SIDE JUDGE**

Article 1   The Side Judge will operate on the same side of the field as the Head Linesman, 20 yards deep.

Article 2   The Side Judge shall count the number of defensive players on the field at the snap.

Article 3   He shall be responsible for all eligible receivers on his side of the field.

Article 4   After receivers have cleared line of scrimmage, the Side Judge will concentrate on action in the area between the Umpire and Back Judge.

Article 5   In addition to the specified use of the whistle by all officials (15-1-4), the Side Judge is also to use his whistle when upon his positive knowledge he knows:

(a) that ball is dead;
(b) that time is out;
(c) that time is out at the end of a down, during which a foul was signaled by a marker, no whistle has sounded in such cases; and

> (d) that even in the presence of a whistle up or down field, he is to sound his whistle when players are some distance from such signal. This will help prevent dead-ball fouls.

Article 6 The Side Judge will assist Referee in decisions involving any catching, recovery, out-of-bounds spot, or illegal touching of a loose ball after it has crossed the scrimmage line, and particularly so for such actions that are out of the range of the Head Linesman and Umpire.

Article 7 The Side Judge will line up in a position laterally from the Umpire on field goals and Try-kick attempts.

Section 8 **BACK JUDGE**

Article 1 The Back Judge is primarily responsible in regard to: covering kicks from scrimmage (unless a Try-kick) or forward passes crossing the defensive goal line and all such loose balls, out of the range of Umpire, Field Judge, and Linesman, noting an illegal substitution or withdrawal during dead ball with time in (see 5-2-1-Notes), and a foul signalled by a flag or cap during down. He will count defensive team.

Article 2 He is to time the intermission between the two periods of each half (4-1-2), the length of all team time outs (4-3-4-S.N. 1 and 2), and the 40/25 seconds permitted Team A to put ball in play (4-3-10-S.N. 1). He is to utilize the 40/25 second clock provided for by the home team. If this clock is inoperative he should take over the official timing of the 40/25 seconds on the field.

Article 3 In addition to the specified use of the whistle by all officials (15-1-4), the Back Judge is also to use his whistle, when upon his own positive knowledge he knows:

(a) that ball is dead;
(b) time is out; or

(c) time is out at end of down, during which a foul was signalled by a flag or cap, and no whistle has sounded in such cases.

Even in the presence of a whistle upfield, he is to sound his when downfield players are some distance away from such signal, and in order to prevent dead-ball fouls. He should be particularly alert for item (c).

Article 4   He shall assist the Referee in decisions involving any catching, recovery, out-of-bounds spot, or illegal touching of a loose ball after it has crossed the scrimmage line and particularly so for such actions as are out of the range of the Field Judge, Linesman, and Umpire. See 15-1-11-S.N. 1. He should count the defensive players on the field at the snap.

Article 5   The Back Judge has the absolute responsibility:

(a) to instruct kicker and/or placekicker that "kickoff" must be made by placekick or dropkick.
(b) that the height of the tee (artificial or natural) used for the kickoff conforms to the governing rules.

Note: He is to notify the visiting team at least five minutes before the start of the second half.

Section 9   **INSTANT REPLAY**

For the 2006, 2007, and 2008 seasons, the League will employ a system of Referee Replay Review to aid officiating for reviewable plays as defined below. Prior to the two-minute warning of each half, a Coaches' Challenge System will be in effect. After the two-minute warning of each half, and throughout any overtime period, a Referee Review will be initiated by a Replay Assistant from a Replay Booth comparable to the location of the coaches' booth or Press Box. The following procedures will be used:

Coaches' Challenge. In each game, a team will be permitted two challenges that will initiate Referee Replay Reviews. Each challenge will require the use of a team time out. If a challenge is upheld, the time out will be restored to the challenging team. A challenge will only be restored if a team is successful on both of its challenges, in which case it shall be awarded a third challenge, but a fourth challenge will not be permitted under any circumstances. No challenges will be recognized from a team that has exhausted its time outs. A team that is out of time outs or has used all of its available challenges may not attempt to initiate an additional challenge.

Penalty: For initiating a challenge when all of a team's time outs have been exhausted or when all of its available challenges have been used: Loss of 15 yards.

Replay Assistant's Request for Review. After the two-minute warning of each half, and throughout any overtime period, any Referee Review will be initiated by a Replay Assistant. There is no limit to the number of Referee Reviews that may be initiated by the Replay Assistant. His ability to initiate a review will be unrelated to the number of time outs that either team has remaining, and no time out will be charged for any review initiated by the Replay Assistant.

Reviews by Referee. All Replay Reviews will be conducted by the Referee on a field-level monitor after consultation with the other covering official(s), prior to review. A decision will be reversed only when the Referee has indisputable visual evidence available to him that warrants the change.

<u>**Time Limit.**</u> <u>For the 2006 season only, each review will be a maximum of 60 seconds in length, timed from</u>

when the Referee begins his review of the replay at the field-level monitor.

Reviewable Plays. The Replay System will cover the following play situations only:

(a) Plays governed by side line, goal line, end zone, and end line:

1. Scoring plays, including a runner breaking the plane of the goal line.
2. Pass complete/incomplete/intercepted at side line, goal line, end zone, and end line.
3. Runner/receiver in or out of bounds.
4. Recovery of loose ball in or out of bounds.

(b) Passing Plays:

1. Pass ruled complete/incomplete/intercepted in the field of play.
2. Touching of a forward pass by an ineligible receiver.
3. Touching of a forward pass by a defensive player.
4. Quarterback (passer) forward pass or fumble.
5. Illegal forward pass beyond line of scrimmage.
6. Illegal forward pass after change of possession.
7. Forward or backward pass thrown from behind line of scrimmage.

(c) Other Detectable Infractions:

1. Runner ruled not down by defensive contact.
2. Runner ruled down by defensive contact when the recovery of a fumble by an opponent or a teammate occurs during the continuing action of the play.

Note 1: If the ruling of down-by-contact is changed, the ball belongs to the recovering player at the spot of the recovery of the fumble, and any advance is nullified.

Note 2: Continuing action is any action that occurs through the recovery of the fumble.

Note 3: If the Referee does not have indisputable visual evidence as to which player recovered the fumble, the ruling of down-by-contact will stand.

Note 4: This does not apply to quarterback pass/fumbles, complete/incomplete passes, or the ruling of forward progress.

3. *Forward progress with respect to a first down.*
4. *Touching of a kick.*
5. *Number of players on the field.*

Note: Non-reviewable plays include but are not limited to:

1. *Status of the clock*
2. *Proper down*
3. *Penalty administration*
4. *Runner ruled down by defensive contact (not involving fumbles)*
5. *Forward progress not relating to first down or goal line*
6. *Forceouts*
7. *Recovery of loose ball in the field of play*
8. *Field goals*
9. *Inadvertent whistle*

Sudden-Death
Procedures

Rule 16

Sudden-Death Procedures

Section 1 **SUDDEN-DEATH PROCEDURES**

Article 1 The sudden-death system of determining the winner shall prevail when the score is tied at the end of the regulation playing time of all NFL games. Under this system, the team scoring first during overtime play herein provided for, shall be the winner of the game and the game is automatically ended upon any score (including a safety) or when a score is awarded by the Referee for a palpably unfair act.

Article 2 At the end of regulation playing time, the Referee shall immediately toss a coin at the center of the field, in accordance with rules pertaining to a usual pregame toss (4-2-1). The visiting team captain is to again call the toss.

Article 3 Following a three-minute intermission after the end of regular game, play shall continue by 15-minute periods with a two-minute intermission between each such overtime period with no halftime intermission.

Exception: Preseason and regular-season league games shall have a maximum of one 15-minute period with the rule for two time outs instead of three as in a regular game and include the general provisions for the fourth quarter of a regular game.

At the end of each extra 15-minute period, starting with the end of the first one, teams must change goals in accordance with rule 4-2-2. Disqualified player(s) may not re-enter during overtime period(s).

Article 4 During any intermission or team time out a player may leave the field.

Article 5   If there is an excess time out during the first and second, third and fourth, etc., extra periods, the usual rules shall apply (4-3-3 to 7).

Article 6   Near the end of any period or during the last two (2) minutes of the second, fourth, etc., extra periods, the usual rules in regard to attempts to conserve time shall apply (4-3-10 and 5-2-1).

The rules for time outs shall be the same as in a regular game, including the last two minutes of the second and fourth quarters.

Article 7   The clock operator shall time all extra 15-minute periods (4-3-1). The Back Judge shall time the three- and two-minute intermissions, and is to sound his whistle 30 seconds before the expiration of each intermission. The Referee shall sound his whistle for play to start, immediately upon the Back Judge's signal. See 4-3-9 and 4-3-10-S.N.

Article 8   Except as specifically provided for above, all other general and specific rules shall apply during any extra period.

Emergencies,
Unfair Acts

Rule 17

Emergencies, Unfair Acts

Section 1   EMERGENCIES

Article 1   If any non-player, including photographers, reporters, employees, police, or spectators, enters the field of play or end zones, and in the judgment of an official said party or parties interfere with the play, the Referee, after consulting his crew (12-3-3 and 15-1-6), shall enforce any such penalty or score as the interference warrants.

Article 2   If spectators enter the field and/or interfere with the progress of the game in such a manner that in the opinion of the Referee the game cannot continue, he shall declare time out. In such a case he shall record the number of the down, distance to be gained, and position of ball on field. He shall also secure from the Line Judge the playing time remaining and record it. He shall then order the home club, through its management, to have the field cleared, and when it is cleared and order restored and the safety of the spectators, players, and officials is assured to the satisfaction of the Referee, the game must continue even if it is necessary to use lights.

Article 3   If the game must be called due to a state or municipal law, or by darkness if no lights are available, an immediate report shall be made to the Commissioner by the home club, visiting club, and officials. On receipt of all reports the Commissioner shall make a decision which will be final.

Article 4   The NFL affirms the position that in most circumstances all regular-season and postseason games should be played to their conclusions. If, in the opinion of appropriate League authorities, it is impossible to begin or continue a game due to an emergency, or a game is deemed to be imminently threatened by any such emergency (e.g., severely inclement weather, lightning, flooding, power failure), the following procedures (Articles 5 through 11) will serve as guidelines for the Commissioner and/or his duly appointed representatives. The Commissioner has the authority to review the circumstances of each emergency and to adjust the following procedures in whatever manner he deems appropriate. If, in the Commissioner's opinion, it is reasonable to project that the resumption of an interrupted game would not change its ultimate result or adversely affect any other inter-team competitive issue, he is empowered to terminate the game.

Article 5   The League employees vested with the authority to define emergencies under these procedures are the Commissioner, designated representatives from his League office staff, and the game Referee. In those instances where neither the Commissioner nor his designated representative is in attendance at a game, the Referee will have sole authority; provided, however, that if a Referee delays the beginning of or interrupts a game for a significant period of time due to an emergency, he must make every effort to contact the Commissioner or the Commissioner's designated representative for consultation. In all cases of significant delay, the League authorities will consult with the management of the participating clubs and will attempt to obtain appropriate information from outside sources, if applicable (e.g., weather bureau, police).

Article 6   If, because of an emergency, a regular-season or postseason game is not started at its scheduled time and cannot be played at any later time that same day, the game nevertheless must be played on a subsequent date to be determined by the Commissioner.

Article 7   If there is deemed to be a threat of an emergency that may occur during the playing of a game (e.g., an incoming tropical storm), the starting time of such game will not be moved to an earlier time unless there is clearly sufficient time to make an orderly change.

Article 8   If, under emergency circumstances, an interrupted regular-season or postseason game cannot be completed on the same day, such game will be rescheduled by the Commissioner and resumed at that point.

Article 9   In instances under these emergency procedures which require the Commissioner to reschedule a regular-season game, he will make every effort to set the game for no later than two days after its originally scheduled date, and he will attempt to schedule the game at its original site. If unable to do so, he will schedule it at the nearest available facility. If it is impossible to schedule the game within two days after its original date, the Commissioner will attempt to schedule it on the Tuesday of the next calendar week in which the two involved clubs play other clubs (or each other). Further, the Commissioner will keep in mind the potential for competitive inequities if one or both of the involved clubs has already been scheduled for a game following the Tuesday of that week (e.g., Thanksgiving).

Article 10   If an emergency interrupts a postseason game and such game cannot be resumed on that same date, the Commissioner will make every effort to arrange for its completion as soon as possible. If unable to schedule the game at the same site, he will select an appropriate alternate site. He will terminate the game short of completion only if in his judgment the continuation of the game would not be normally expected to alter the ultimate result.

Article 11   In all instances where a game is resumed after interruption, either on the same date or a subsequent date, the resumption will begin at the point at which the game was interrupted. At the time of interruption, the Referee will call time out and he will make a record of the following: the team possessing the ball, the direction in which its offense was headed, position of the ball on the field, down, distance, period, time remaining in the period, and any other pertinent information required for an efficient and equitable resumption of play.

Section 2   EXTRAORDINARILY UNFAIR ACTS

Article 1   The Commissioner has the sole authority to investigate and take appropriate disciplinary and/or corrective measures if any club action, non-participant interference, or calamity occurs in an NFL game which he deems so extraordinarily unfair or outside the accepted tactics encountered in professional football that such action has a major effect on the result of the game.

Article 2   The authority and measures provided for in this entire Section 2 do not constitute a protest machinery for NFL clubs to avail themselves of in the event a dispute arises over the result of a game. The investigation called for in this Section 2 will be conducted solely on the Commissioner's initiative to review an act or occurrence that he deems so extraordinary or unfair that the result of the game in question would be inequitable to one of the participating teams. The Commissioner will not apply his authority in cases of complaints by clubs concerning judgmental errors or routine errors of omission by game officials. Games involving such complaints will continue to stand as completed.

Article 3 The Commissioner's powers under this Section 2 include the imposition of monetary fines and draft-choice forfeitures, suspension of persons involved in unfair acts, and, if appropriate, the reversal of a game's result or the rescheduling of a game, either from the beginning or from the point at which the extraordinary act occurred. In the event of rescheduling a game, the Commissioner will be guided by the procedures specified in Rule 17, Section 1, Articles 5 through 11, above. In all cases, the Commissioner will conduct a full investigation, including the opportunity for hearings, use of game videotape, and any other procedure he deems appropriate.

Guidelines
for Captains

Rule 18

Guidelines for Captains

Section 1 **GUIDELINES FOR CAPTAINS**

Article 1 One hour and thirty minutes prior to kickoff: Respective coaches designate the captain(s)—a maximum of six per team.

Article 2 Coin toss:

(a) Up to six captains per team can participate in the coin-toss ceremony; only one captain from the visiting team (or captain designated by Referee if there is no home team) can declare the choice of coin toss.

(b) The team that won the toss may then have only one captain declare its option.

(c) The team that lost the coin toss may then have only one captain declare its option.

Article 3 Choice on penalty option: Only one captain is permitted to indicate the team's penalty option.

Article 4 Change of captains:

(a) The coach has prerogative of informing Referee when he wishes to make a change in team captains; or

(b) A captain who is leaving can inform the Referee which player will act as captain in his place when he is substituted for; or

(c) When a captain leaves the game, the incoming substitute is permitted to inform the Referee which player the respective coach has designated as captain.

Note: A captain on the field has no authority to request a change of fellow team captain when that captain remains on the field.

Penalty
Summary

Distance Penalties

Loss of Five Yards

Each time out in each half being in excess of three unless
not notified or unless a fourth time out for injured player
as specified (see charged time out penalties) ....4-3-5, and 6

Delay of game, i.e.,

exceeding 40/25 seconds in putting ball in play 4-3-9

failing to play immediately when ordered 4-3-9

repeatedly snapping ball before referee can assume
normal position ....4-3-9 and 7-3-3-c-2

runner repeatedly attempting to advance when
securely held 4-3-9

runner remaining on ball or opponent remaining
on runner to consume time 4-3-9

undue delay in assembling after a time out 4-3-9

repeatedly entering neutral zone when not
otherwise encroaching 4-3-9

defense prior to snap...4-3-9

unduly delaying establishment of neutral zone
especially during time in 4-3-9

illegal return 5-1-5

kickers advancing recovered kick (not behind line)
causes delay ....4-3-9 and 9-1-4

substituting while ball is in play unless
interference ....4-3-9 and 12-3-1

contacting snapper or ball 7-3-5

catcher unduly advancing after fair catch signal .....4-3-9 and 10-1-2

attempting to conserve time near end of period,
especially during last two minutes of half (also stop or
not to stop game clock to nullify) 4-3-10

more than eleven players on field during play 5-1-1

Running into kicker behind his line (not roughing) 12-2-6

Incidental grasp of face mask 12-2-5

Loss of 10 Yards

Pass interference by team A 8-2-5

Tripping, holding, illegal use of hands,
arms or body on offense 12-1-4

Assisting runner 12-1-1

Batting or punching ball, when loose (unless a pass),
towards opponents' goal line or in any
direction if in end zone...12-1-8

Illegally kicking ball 12-1-9

Loss of 15 Yards

Not being ready to start each half on scheduled time 4-1-5

Interfering with fair catch (and catch awarded) 10-1-4

Tackling or blocking maker of a fair catch or
avoidable running into 10-1-5

Head slap 12-2-2

Striking, kneeing, and kicking (also disqualification) 12-2-1

Striking an opponent on head, neck, or face
with palm of hands 12-2-3

Striking opponent below shoulders with forearm
or elbow by turning or pivoting 12-2-4

Twisting, turning, or pulling of opponent's face mask 12-2-5

Blocking below waist on kicks and change of possession 12-2-13

Roughing the kicker 12-2-6

Falling on or piling on a prostrate player 12-2-7

Unnecessary roughness (also disqualification
when flagrant), i.e.,

    striking an opponent above knee with foot or shin 12-2-8

    tackling runner who is out of bounds 12-2-8

Loss of Half Distance to Goal Line

Ball Placed on 1-Yard Line

Withdrawal Penalties

Disqualification Penalties

Disqualification always occurs in combination with
a 15-yard penalty. Exceptions to distance penalties:

Loss of 15 Yards

Loss of Ball Penalties

Disqualification for Entire Game

Charged Time Out Penalties

Time Penalty

Replay Penalties

Scoring Penalties

Try Awarded

Score Awarded

Touchdown Awarded

Safety

Intentional grounding in own end zone......................................8-3-1

Making a forward pass (not from scrimmage)
from within passer's end zone..................................8-1-1 and 14-1-11

Score Not Allowed

Offending team scores after foul during down in which
time expires for half (also no extension of time)......................4-3-11

Unsuccessful Try

Attempted kick ceasing to be in play.......................................11-3-1

Team A committing foul during a Try which
would ordinarily result:

    in loss of down or in a touchback...11-3-3

    in loss of ball in field of play (not during a kick) 11-3-3

    B recovering ball 11-3-5

New Series Penalties

B committing a foul during play from scrimmage
giving A first down irrespective of distance penalty.................14-8-5

B committing a foul not giving A first down unless
enforcement places ball in advance of necessary
line, i.e.,

    excess time out..4-3-6

    delay of game 4-3-9

    illegal substitution..5-2-1

    illegal equipment (suspension) 5-3-1

    encroaching on neutral zone or being offside 7-2-2

    B touching snapper or ball 7-3-5

B interfering in field of play with a pass from
behind line (distance penalty in addition when
personal foul) ....8-2-5 and 12-2-1

Combination Penalties

Loss of Down and Five

Making a forward pass from scrimmage from
beyond the line..8-1-1

Loss of Down and 10

Intentionally grounds pass (from behind line) 8-3-1

Loss of Ball and 15

Interfering with a possible fair catch in field of
play (also fair catch)..10-1-4

Touchback

Kickers illegally touching kick (not free kick) in
receiver's end zone..9-1-4

Fair catch interfering or running into maker
of in receiver's end zone...10-1-5

Score, Distance, or Disqualification

Referee makes equitable ruling..15-2-1

    player committing palpably
    unfair act...12-3-3

    non-player committing
    palpably unfair act...13-1-7

Miscellaneous Situations

Safety

Ball in possession of team behind or out of
bounds behind own goal line and impetus
which sent it in touch came from:

    Player of that team (unless pass violation by A is enforced
    from previous spot)—Safety.....................................11-4-1 and 2

Kickoff Out of Bounds Between Goal Lines

Receiver's ball at inbounds spot when last touched
by them...6-3-1

Receiver's ball 30 yards from previous spot.................................6-3-1

Ball Remains Dead

Fouls relating to the start of a down (ball not
being in play even if the action begins) 14-6

Actions which delay game ....4-3-9 and 10

Snapping before referee assumes normal position 7-3-3

Ball Dead Immediately

Committing acts designed to consume time 4-3-10

Kickers recovering a short free kick..6-2-2

Down ending because of and at the time of a
foul, i.e.,
    any forward pass becoming incomplete anywhere 8-1-5

Kickers advancing after recovery of a scrimmage
kick unless behind line other than a
try-kick (9-1-4) ....9-1-6 and 11-3-5

Any kick touching receiver's goal post or cross bar
unless scoring field goal ....6-3-2; 9-1-14; and 11-6-1

Official sounding whistle (even when
accidental) 7-4-3

Any receiver catching after fair catch signal unless
touched in flight by kickers..10-1-2

Penalty Enforced From Goal Line

Defense fouling and spot of enforcement is
behind goal line of offense 14-1-11

Runner crosses opponent's goal line and spot of
enforcing foul by teammate during run is behind
defense goal line 14-1-12

Penalty Enforced on Next Free Kick

A team scoring and opponents commit a personal
or unsportsmanlike conduct foul or a palpably
unfair act, during down 14-1-14

Official
Signals

1

**TOUCHDOWN,
FIELD GOAL, OR
SUCCESSFUL TRY**
Both arms extended
above head.

2

SAFETY
Palms together
above head.

3

FIRST DOWN
Arm pointed toward
defensive team's goal.

4

**CROWD NOISE, DEAD BALL, OR
NEUTRAL ZONE ESTABLISHED**
One arm above head with an
open hand. With fist closed:
FOURTH DOWN.

5

**BALL ILLEGALLY TOUCHED,
KICKED,
OR BATTED**
Fingertips tap both
shoulders.

6

TIME OUT
Hands crisscrossed above
head. Same signal followed
by placing one hand on top
of cap: **REFEREE'S TIME OUT.**
Same signal followed by
arm swung at side:
TOUCHBACK.

7

NO TIME OUT OR TIME IN WITH WHISTLE
Full arm circled to simulate moving clock.

8

DELAY OF GAME, OFFENSE/DEFENSE, OR EXCESS TIME OUT
Folded arms.

9

FALSE START, ILLEGAL FORMATION, KICKOFF OR SAFETY KICK OUT OF BOUNDS, OR KICKING TEAM PLAYER VOLUNTARILY OUT OF BOUNDS DURING A PUNT
Forearms rotated over and over in front of body.

10

PERSONAL FOUL
One wrist striking the other above head. Same signal followed by swinging leg: **ROUGHING KICKER**. Same signal followed by raised arm swinging forward: **ROUGHING PASSER**. Same signal followed by grasping face mask: **MAJOR FACE MASK**.

11

HOLDING
Grasping one wrist, the fist clenched, in front of chest.

12

ILLEGAL USE OF HANDS, ARMS, OR BODY
Grasping one wrist, the hand open and facing forward, in front of chest.

13

PENALTY REFUSED, INCOMPLETE PASS, PLAY OVER, OR MISSED GOAL
Hands shifted in horizontal plane.

14

PASS JUGGLED INBOUNDS AND CAUGHT OUT OF BOUNDS
Hands up and down in front of chest (following incomplete pass signal).

15

ILLEGAL FORWARD PASS
One hand waved behind back followed by loss of down signal (23) when appropiate.

16

INTENTIONAL GROUNDING OF PASS
Parallel arms waved in a diagonal plane across body. Followed by loss of down signal (23).

17

INTERFERENCE WITH FORWARD PASS OR FAIR CATCH
Hands open and extended forward from shoulders with hands vertical.

18

INVALID FAIR CATCH SIGNAL
One hand waved above head.

19

INELIGIBLE RECEIVER OR INELIGIBLE MEMBER OF KICKING TEAM DOWNFIELD
Right hand touching top of cap.

20

ILLEGAL CONTACT
One open hand extended forward.

21

OFFSIDE, ENCROACHMENT, OR NEUTRAL ZONE INFRACTION
Hands on hips.

22

ILLEGAL MOTION AT SNAP
Horizontal arc with one hand.

23

LOSS OF DOWN
Both hands held behind head.

24

INTERLOCKING INTERFERENCE, PUSHING, OR HELPING RUNNER
Pushing movement of hands to front with arms downward.

25
TOUCHING A FORWARD PASS OR SCRIMMAGE KICK
Diagonal motion of one hand across another.

26
UNSPORTSMANLIKE CONDUCT
Arms outstretched, palms down.

27
ILLEGAL CUT
Both hands striking front of thigh. **ILLEGAL BLOCK BELOW THE WAIST:** One hand striking front of thigh preceded by personal foul signal (10). **CHOP BLOCK:** Both hands striking side of thighs preceded by personal foul signal (10). **CLIPPING:** One hand striking back of calf preceded by personal foul signal (10).

28
ILLEGAL CRACKBACK
Strike of an open right hand against the right mid thigh preceded by personal foul signal (10).

29
PLAYER DISQUALIFIED
Ejection signal.

30
TRIPPING
Repeated action of right foot in back of left heel.

31

**UNCATCHABLE
FORWARD PASS**

Palm of right hand held
parallel to ground above
head and moved back
and forth.

32

**ILLEGAL SUBSTITUTION,
12 MEN IN OFFENSIVE
HUDDLE, OR TOO MANY MEN
ON THE FIELD**

Both hands on top of head.

33

FACE MASK

Grasping mask with one
hand.

34

ILLEGAL SHIFT

Horizontal arcs with two
hands.

35

**RESET PLAY CLOCK –
25 SECONDS**

Pump one arm vertically.

36

**RESET PLAY CLOCK –
40 SECONDS**

Pump two arms vertically.